Ethical Living through Stories

Encounters with *Adab*

Wen-chin Ouyang

I.B. TAURIS

LONDON • NEW YORK • OXFORD • NEW DELHI • SYDNEY

In association with
The Institute of Ismaili Studies
LONDON, 2025

I.B. TAURIS
Bloomsbury Publishing Plc
50 Bedford Square, London, WC1B 3DP, UK
1385 Broadway, New York, NY 10018, USA
29 Earlsfort Terrace, Dublin 2, Ireland

In association with The Institute of Ismaili Studies
Aga Khan Centre, 10 Handyside Street, London N1C 4DN
www.iis.ac.uk

BLOOMSBURY, I.B. TAURIS and the I.B. Tauris logo are
trademarks of Bloomsbury Publishing Plc

First published in Great Britain 2025

A catalogue record for this book is available from the British Library.

A catalog record for this book is available from the Library of Congress.

ISBN: PB: 978-0-7556-5749-0
       ePDF: 978-0-7556-5751-3
       eBook: 978-0-7556-5750-6

Series: World of Islam

Typeset by RefineCatch Limited, Bungay, Suffolk
Printed and bound in Great Britain

For product safety related questions contact productsafety@bloomsbury.com

To find out more about our authors and books visit
www.bloomsbury.com and sign up for our newsletters.

Contents

Note on the Text   v

Introduction   1

Chapter 1. Virtuous City: Sovereign, Courtier,
            Subject   21

Chapter 2. Heroic Family: Love, Desire,
            Marriage   52

Chapter 3. Harmonious Community: Fathers
            and Mothers, Sons and Daughters   78

Chapter 4. Alternative Society: The Fellowship
            of Men and Women   99

Chapter 5. *Joie de Vivre*: Life is a Banquet   124

Chapter 6. Heaven on Earth: Storytelling and
            Meanings of Life   147

Conclusion   178

Glossary   184

Notes   189

Further Reading and Viewing   195

List of Illustrations   201

Index   205

Note on the Text

In the interest of readability, diacritics for trans-literated words have been limited to the ayn (') and the hamza (') where they occur in the middle of a word. All dates are Common Era, unless otherwise indicated. English quotations from the Qur'an are based on Muhammad Abdel Haleem, tr., *The Qur'an: A new translation* (Oxford, 2004). Stories from the *Thousand and One Nights* draw on Hussein Haddawy, tr., *The Arabian Nights: Based on the Text Edited by Muhsin Mahdi* (New York, 1990), unless stated otherwise. Supplementary material related to the content of the book is available on the IIS website: www.iis.ac.uk.

Previous publications by the author on which the book is based

Ouyang, Wen-Chin. 'Romancing the Epic: *'Umar al-Nu'man* as Narrative of Empowerment'. *Arabic and Middle Eastern Literatures* 3, 1 (2000), pp. 5–18.

——. 'The Epical Turn of Romance: Love in the Narrative of 'Umar al-Nu'mān'. *Oriente Moderno* 19, 1 (2002), pp. 485–504.

——. 'Metamorphoses of Scheherazade in Literature and Film'. *Bulletin of SOAS* 66, 3 (2003), pp. 402–418.

——. 'Whose Story Is It? Sindbad the Sailor in Literature and Film'. *Middle Eastern Literatures* 7, 2 (2004), pp. 133–147.

———. 'Utopian Fantasy or Dystopian Nightmare: Trajectories of Desire in Classical Arabic and Chinese Fiction'. In *Le repertoire narrative arabe medieval: transmission et ouverture*, ed. Aboubakr Chraibi, Frederic Bauden and Antonella Ghersetti. Geneva: Droz, 2008, pp. 323–351.

———. 'An Ethical Underworld?: Legendary Con Artists in Arabic Vernacular Fiction'. *Islamic Legends*, special issue of *Oriente Moderno* LXXXIX, ed. Giovanni Canova (2009), pp. 407–424.

———. 'Intertextuality and Transformation: Collective Memory in Arabic and Chinese Narratives of History' (in Arabic). *Alif: A Journal of Comparative Poetics* 34 (2014), pp. 109–135.

———. 'Male Friendship in Arabic and Chinese Cultures' (in Arabic). *Alif: A Journal of Comparative Poetics* 36 (2015), pp. 145–172.

———. 'Solomon's Ring in the Arabic Literary Imaginary'. In *The Qur'an and Adab: The Shaping of Literary Traditions in Classical Islam*, ed. Nuha Al-Shaar. Oxford: Oxford University Press in association with the Institute of Ismaili Studies, 2017, pp. 433–471.

———. 'A Hairy State of Mind: Creativity in the Arabic Literary Imaginary'. *Al-Masaq: Journal of Medieval Mediterranean* 30, 1 (2018), pp. 71–89.

———. 'Trickster Jester: On humour, word play and laughter in the *Arabian Nights*'. In *Festschrift zum 65. Geburtstag von Ulrich Marzolph Vol. 1*, ed. Regina Bendix and Dorothy Noyes. Dortmund: Verlag für Orientkunde, 2018, pp. 32–58.

———. '*The Arabian Nights* in Chinese and English Translations: Differing Patterns of Cultural Encounter and World Literature'. In *World Literature in Motion: Institution, Recognition, Location*, ed. Flair Donglai Shi and Gareth Guangmin Tan. Stuttgart: Ibidem Verlag, 2020, pp. 435–474.

———. 'Multilingualism and Creativity in World Literature'. In *Creative Multilingualism: A Manifesto*, ed. Katrin Kohl et al. AHRC-funded

OWRI Programme. Open Book Publishers, 2020, pp. 109–130. https://doi.org/10.11647/OBP.0206

——. 'The Silk Roads of World Literature'. In *The Cambridge History of World Literature*, Vol. 1, ed. Debjani Ganguly. Cambridge: Cambridge University Press, 2021, pp. 63–79.

——. 'Harun al-Rashid in Premodern Arabic Literary Imaginary: Ideology of Monogamy, Harem Politics and Court Intrigues'. In *The Historian of Islam at Work: Essays in Honor of Hugh N. Kennedy*, ed. Maaiko van Berkel and Letizia Osti. Leiden: Brill, 2022), pp. 340–355.

——. 'Coincidence and Entanglement: Wonder and Framing in *The Thousand and One Nights*'. *Journal of Arabic and Islamic Studies* 24, 1 (2024), pp. 189–208.

——. 'The *Thousand and One Nights* and Rethinking Arabic Literature'. Approaches to Teaching *The Thousand and One Nights* (Approaches to Teaching World Literature), ed. Paulo Horta. Approaches to Teaching World Literature. New York: Modern Languages Association of America, 2023, pp. 40–47.

Introduction

Multilingual Readings and Comparative Literature: The Life of a Taiwanese in Libya

I cannot remember when I started reading or in which language, but stories have filled my head since I was a child in Libya. My family moved from Taiwan to Libya in 1964 as a part of the Republic of China's diplomatic mission. We lived in Gharyan for six years before moving north to Tripoli in 1969. Until I was eighteen, I went to Libyan schools during the day, took English lessons at the Language Institute founded by the British in the early evenings, and studied Chinese at the Taiwanese community school over the weekends. Reading stories was my favourite pastime.

The *Thousand and One Nights* adapted for children arrived at our house in a stack of Chinese books my parents borrowed from friends. Among them were the heroic tales of three generations of the Xue military family during the Tang Dynasty, *La Dame aux Camélias* (by Alexandre Dumas fils), Sherlock Holmes, Arsène Lupin, and the eighteenth-century Chinese detective novel *Shi Gongan*. While I admired the loyalty and heroism of the Xue

Figure 1. 19th-century edition of an Urdu translation of the *Thousand and One Nights*, including the marginalia in volume three.

generals, the intelligence and resourcefulness of Holmes, Lupin and Shi, and the romance in Dumas, I wanted more than anything to be Sindbad the Sailor, to travel around the world unencumbered by worldly possessions, and to go on pioneering adventures.

Reading in Arabic and English came later, after we moved to Tripoli. I began with the Arabic stories of the prophets and of the heroes of Islam, especially those by Jurji Zaydan, and then I slowly moved on to contemporary novels, such as science fiction by Mustafa Mahmud and romantic tales by Ihsan ʿAbd al-Quddus and Yusuf al-Sibaʿi. Between the ages of fifteen and eighteen, I discovered Charles Dickens, first in Arabic, then in English at the Ferjiani bookshop, and my journey into English storytelling began. Being multilingual, I read books in whichever language I found them. Just as I read Dickens in Arabic first, I read Jane Austen's *Pride and Prejudice* and Emily Brontë's *Wuthering Heights* in Chinese before reading them in English. Similarly, I read Dostoyevsky's *Crime and Punishment* in Arabic but Tolstoy's *Anna Karenina* and *War and Peace* in English and Romain Rolland's *Jean-Christophe* in Chinese.

The world I wove together from the stories I read in three languages was seamlessly coherent. The stories were all about what it is to be human, and how to live as humans. The heroes and heroines in historical romances cut the same chivalrous figures. They were brave, loyal and adventurous. Their sovereigns were all magnanimous, just, and kind. On the contrary, the villainous enemies of those heroes were evil, corrupt, selfish, and greedy. I drew comparisons between the different cultures: General Xue was Khalid b. al-Walid, Emperor Taizong of Tang was Harun al-Rashid, and the female protagonists in the works of Austen and Brontë possessed the same intelligence, will and defiance as their predecessors in the *Thousand and One Nights* as well as in Chinese historical and chivalric romances. My reading during my university years deepened my sense that literary traditions around the world have much in common. It never occurred to me that the languages in which they are written would present impediments to my youthful dreams of studying Arabic–Chinese comparative literature.

Adab and *Wen*: Arabic and Chinese Literatures

Throughout my career as a literary scholar I have looked for ways to bring Arabic and Chinese literatures together in discussions of literariness and aesthetics without flouting the disciplinary foundations of both literary studies and comparative literature, but also without becoming bogged down by their imaginings of what language is, how it maps sovereign literary and cultural worlds, and plausible literary and comparative studies. Influence and parallel studies aside, there are many possible avenues for comparison. One is to bring critical perspectives derived from the study of the two literatures to bear on each other. The fluidity of movement among the various registers of the Chinese languages can be useful for delineating an alternative Arabic literary history.

The Arabic literary canon has until very recently been defined as what is written and by the grammaticality of its language. The classical Arabic language is imagined as sovereign. Poetry and story transmitted in any other Arabic register were not allowed a place in Arabic literary history or a role in the development of Arabic literature. Stories expressed in middle Arabic, such as the *Nights* and the popular epic cycles (known as *sira sha'biyya*), or in colloquial poems and tales, were relegated to a separate sphere of oral folklore.

Such a stark distinction between the classical and the folk is arguably the effect of how we have been reading Arabic poetry and story for centuries. The tradition of reading we have inherited, and perhaps even reinvented in the nineteenth century, is informed by a set of conceptual categories that organize literary production and critical reception in discrete genres according to a language hierarchy. It conceals the conversations that take place among the poems and stories cast in different registers of the Arabic language and genres of Arabic storytelling and writing. Thus, the *Thousand and One Nights* and Arabic epics, for example, recorded in the vernacular or colloquial Arabic with no fixed text or named author, have been classified as folk or popular literature and excluded from discussions of classical Arabic *adab*.

The Chinese tradition of reading does not follow a similar trajectory. Rather, it shows dialogue across varying registers and genres. Poetic forms develop and change, and new ones emerge. A novel refashions material from drama, or vice versa. Stories rewrite history, and folk narratives complement official accounts. Cultural productions based on the word all belong to a field that consists of multifarious fields, activities, and languages. *Adab* in Arabic, like *wen* in Chinese, embraces a plurality of activities expressed in diverse linguistic registers and engaged in manifold dialogues. An Arab man of letters, an *adib*, is a polymath and a public intellectual, just like his Chinese counterpart, a *wenren*, who participates in all cultural activities.

Adab and *wen*, before the two terms acquired the European definition of literature in the nineteenth and twentieth centuries, denoted a culture of engagement with the material conditions of living in all their variety and diversity, including expressions of, contemplations on, and lessons learnt from such an engagement. As such, their content defies categorization. According to the fourteenth-century scholar Ibn Khaldun in the prologue to his history (*Muqaddima*), *adab* is one of the four sciences of the Arabic language, preceded in importance by grammar, lexicography, and style. Ibn Khaldun defines *adab* as an area of intellectual activity (*'ilm*), interested in the effective use of language, particularly in poetry or prose, rather than any particular subject they tackle. Language is at the heart of this exercise, as is our conduct. *Adab*, as Stefan Sperl shows in his comparative analysis of *adab* and *hadith* compendia, comprises the Muslim ethics of living activated in language.[1]

Wen, equally grounded in the cultivation of language and its related activities, is arguably expressive of the Confucian ethics of living.

Working side by side with religion, philosophy and spirituality, *adab* and *wen* have in common a concern with the human condition. Humanity is at the core of their interrogations and reflections. How is a human being distinguished from other living beings? What are human rights, and what responsibilities do humans have towards fellow humans and other living beings based on this difference? How is the human to live as an individual and as a member of a community? This book is about the ethics of living that *adab* embodies but approached through the prism of story. We desperately need *adab* and *wen* to help us navigate the tumult we are experiencing today.

A STORY-TELLER RECITING FROM THE "ARABIAN NIGHTS."
In the background are the ramparts of the Citadel.

Figure 2. A storyteller reciting from the *Arabian Nights* in Cairo. In the background are the ramparts of the Citadel. From Douglas Sladen, 'Oriental Cairo: the city of the *Arabian Nights*'.

Humanity in Crisis: Humanities Under Siege

Inflation, income stagnation, and years of state neglect of the public sector have precipitated a crisis in the humanities. Excellent research has not been able to rescue the humanities from low recruitment at universities, nor prevent funding cuts, redundancies, and the withdrawal of programmes. Many Arabic literature modules at UK universities have been withdrawn since the 2008 financial crisis and the loss of public funding for less-taught languages at universities in the UK, a trajectory expedited by Brexit and Covid. Classical literature has been a devastating casualty. Even modern literature is at risk. Yet, with the continuous wars and armed conflicts in the world, the flight and plight of refugees, the increased violent incidents in virtually every major city, the escalation of cancel culture, environmental crisis, the political fallout in practically every country, and within and beyond the educational sector the real intellectual and moral conundrum generated by AI, social media, and cyber gangsterism, we have never needed literature more than we do today.

Literature, whether we call it *adab* in Arabic or *wen* in Chinese, has for thousands of years been the public sphere in which human beings have worked out the ethics of living for every day, critically reflecting on them during times of crisis and change and bringing them up to date. It is where the lines between the individual and collective, the private and public, and the self and other are drawn. More importantly, each is redefined and refined in accordance with the developments in the material conditions of human living.

We work out and articulate all possible positions and perspectives in literary works and represent nuances of our thought and emotion in such a way as to invite reflection and solicit understanding. This role of literature is indispensable, for example, in demonstrating the impact of the Israel–Palestine conflict on all of us, not only on Palestinians and Israelis. It shows us the consequences of othering, of breaching fundamental human rights, and of ignoring injustice in the Arab world as well as in the Muslim world and the globe at large. More importantly, it shows us where work is needed and how we can perform the task. It tells us we need to decolonise the structure of our thought and conduct, and it can show us how, albeit indirectly. If we treated Palestinians, or any of our potential victims, our others, like ourselves, would we be where we are today?

In this book, I offer an outline of a fundamental code of conduct for every day, structured around the push and pull between love and desire in the Solomon legends and the Harun al-Rashid myths in Arabic works, and as echoed in Chinese *wen*. This code of conduct, proposed in pre-modern Arabic literature and seen through the prism of classical Chinese literature, would usher in a harmonious community in which there is room and a meaningful role for every living being. My account does not encompass all the details of the struggles of quotidian life and the solutions offered by Arabic and Chinese literatures. I focus on the pre-modern, in particular the *Thousand and One Nights*, to show its abiding relevance, and the ways in which that work, in its own discourses on love and desire, teaches the powerful to be reasonable, loving, loyal, magnanimous, responsible, and just. It teaches them to care for those less fortunate and those suffering and, more importantly, to be patient and enduring rather than, for example, resorting to crime and betrayal of their kith and kin.

Our community is our family and friends, and every member deserves our love and care, not our exploitation and violation. This basic code of conduct can be expanded to cover many aspects of our life. Even then, living need not be austere. A proper life need not contradict a good life. We can, and should, enjoy life, even its trials and tribulations, and our attempts at living by or transgressing the very code of conduct we have devised. More importantly, there is an infinitely more wonderous world outside our material world, including our inner life, that is waiting to take us on fantastic adventures.

The Solomon Legends and the Harun al-Rashid Myths: The Ethics of Everyday Living

The biblical King Solomon and the historical Harun al-Rashid (r. 786–809) are two of the most popular characters in storytelling around the

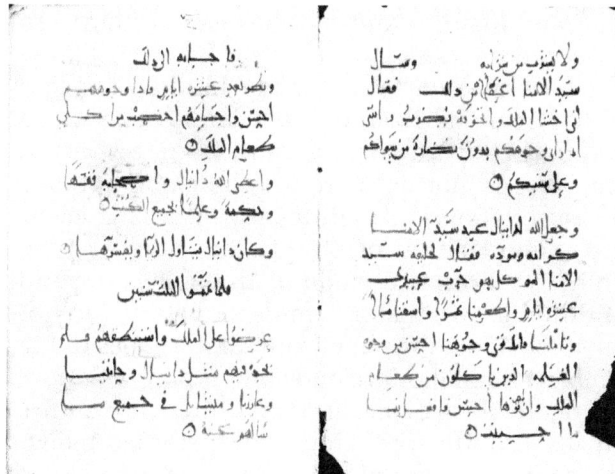

Figure 3. Book of Daniel and Solomon's Proverbs.

world. Their power, the fabulous dominions they established and ruled, and their conduct as man, sovereign, son, brother, father, and husband are all the stuff of storytelling. For centuries, storytellers have spun yarns about their exploits and adventures, from building cities to conquests and founding empires; from holding court and dispensing justice and giving wise counsel to managing wives, concubines, slaves, and sons at home; and from regular tours of their dominions to encounters with impersonators. Information from the earliest accounts has been fashioned into fantastic tales with quotidian details added from an invented life. It is today impossible to separate history and fiction where they are concerned.

The figures of Solomon of biblical folklore and Harun al-Rashid of Islamic anecdotes (*akhbar*) have travelled widely, from the past to the present, not only around the globe but also across religions and cultures as well as languages, texts, and genres of storytelling and writing. They appear in pre-modern Arabic, Islamic and Middle-Eastern history, *adab*, and story, including tales of the prophets, epics and stories of the *Nights*, and in modern and contemporary fiction, taking the form of stories for children, adventure novels and films, religious and historical television dramas, and political allegories.

Such tellings and retellings have over the centuries transformed them from exemplars into myths, structures of knowledge around which generations of storytellers and their audiences have articulated their dreams of an ideal community. This ideal community is at once religious, political, social, and spiritual, located in this world as well as in the hereafter. It thrives on the proper conduct of its every member. Its members inhabit two overlapping networks of political authority and social relations, which are informed by religious teachings and spiritual aspirations.

These legends and myths serve as the site and means for us to define, test, and refine our ethics of living both as individuals and as members of a community. They offer a code of conduct whose contours gain clarity in the human struggle to strike a balance between care for the self and service to others, power and justice, profit and fairness, disorder and order, lawlessness and law, and between discord and harmony. Communal harmony is dependent on the coming together of the political and the social and in fact on how social relations can guide and regulate all forms of power. Family is here the kernel of community. Moreover, in their conversations with each other, these elements extend the human purview to what is beyond the material world of our political and social community.

Chinese cultural and literary expressions are concerned with, and structured around, the meticulously articulated five social relationships in Confucianism, *wulun*, through which they interrogate the individual and collective code of conduct that underpins both familial and communal harmony as well as how its violation leads to disharmony. This conduct, like its counterpart in Arabic culture and literature, is seen as negotiated around love and fidelity between 'sovereign, courtier and subject', 'husband and wife', 'parent and child', 'brother and sister', and 'friends'. This code of conduct takes shape in the dialogues between two concepts: love that is equated with reason, and desire that drives passion. Loyalty of all kinds is born in love and educated by reason, and disloyalty is the result of passion gone awry. Love and reason bring about harmony and desire leads to chaos.

The biblical Solomon, distinguished by his wisdom, has in common with historical Harun al-Rashid absolute power over their dominions and harems, through their wise rule, justice, magnanimity, and skillful management of court and harem intrigues. Leading retinues of humans and angels, genies and demons, and animals, birds, and insects, the Solomon of legend conquers the world and builds a pluriversal empire, has time for love and family, and marries wives and rears sons. Managing a large empire and harem, Harun al-Rashid similarly goes on campaigns and tours around his capital at night to ensure that no injustice is committed in the public and private world under his care.

Their conduct as sovereigns, husbands, brothers, and fathers is at the heart of the ideal community imagined around them. Even their belongings, such as Solomon's signet ring, come to be symbolic of their political and social power and how they held it responsibly, managed its influence on those around him, and deployed it as an instrument of everyday justice, not only at court but also in the harem and the street.

An additional relationship between human and divine underpins the Solomon legends and the Harun al-Rashid myths. Revelations, the Torah, Bible, and Qur'an, inform how the believer should behave as an individual in the community in relation to God in Abrahamic religions. Buddhism and Daoism, quite often intertwined in Chinese culture, carve out a space for contemplation beyond the Confucian social structure and the materiality of living steeped in political power struggles and social climbing.

Whether focused on the future – Paradise in Abrahamic religions, or the present – Nirvana in Buddhism and Dao in Daoism, Arabic and Chinese cultural and literary expressions share an impulse to find freedom from the trappings of the material conditions of living, often translating Paradise, Nirvana, and Dao into a form of spirituality, a search for purpose and meaning of life outside the confines of the political, social, and even religious. Yet this transcendental impulse is equally grounded in the very same quotidian ethics of living. Bringing the Chinese *wulun* into conversation with Arabic storytelling (*qisas*) and literature (*adab*) allows us to clearly see the ways in which the political and social are integrated into the yearning for the divine and the journey through life towards the hereafter.

The changing and differing material conditions of living across multiple temporalities and geographies provide a fertile ground for the worldwide telling and retelling of the Solomon legends and the Harun al-Rashid myths. They fuel a need to update and rework their imaginings of ideal community and the attendant ethics of everyday living. They stimulate new creative renderings of these legends and myths to work out how an individual should conduct oneself in a differently constructed world. How do we work out our relationship with the sovereign of a contemporary democratic nation state around a code of conduct born in the age of empire and Caliphate? What role does new technology play in transforming our experience of the world, our sense of ourselves in relation to others, and our ways of belonging to our community? Do these new communal structures and technologies redefine who we are and our place in family and community? Can we remain firm in our faith while recognizing religions not our own?

Such new developments complicate the processes through which humankind has forever negotiated our ambitions for political power and social standing, and our desire for material wealth and even immortality in the form of both fame and family. These – the eternal struggle between passion and reason, and the rapidly changing material conditions of our living – offer us ample ingredients for the stories we tell about ourselves, adding twists and turns each time we retell them.

These stories are reflections of ourselves. They are the mirror in which we see our good and evil, strengths and weaknesses, selfish desires and altruistic impulses, and our attempts to discipline ourselves and failures to do so. More importantly, we watch the long process through which we try to construct an ideal community only to undermine every step we take and unravel every thread we weave into its fabric.

Humanity is not perfection. Its imperfection is the site of contemplation as well as *joie de vivre*. An ethical life need not be austere, regimented, or dull. On the contrary, the struggle between love and desire in the Solomon legends and the Harun al-Rashid myths, often told with exuberant pleasure and keen humour, takes us on journeys around the world and within ourselves that are filled with adventure, wonder, fun, and even subversion and self-mockery. We can laugh at our foibles with affection, finding relief and joy in the adventures and even the misadventures into which they hurtle us. For without desire there can be no life, and the story of our life is precisely that of taming our desire for power, wealth, and fame for ourselves and our family. Such a desire is natural and integral to humankind, but in excess and without regard for others it becomes a destructive force that puts not only us but also our community under threat.

This book is about the stories we tell of ourselves, our struggles to be good and our hopes for a harmonious community in which we can live a happy and meaningful life. It is also about how we tell these stories and the impact of storytelling on our life aspirations. Structured around the five *wulun* social rela-tions and an additional sixth relation between the divine and the human, each of the six chapters of this book offers a part of the human search for and journey towards an ideal community as well as reflections on the search and how we tell it. The first four chapters are concerned with building an ideal community in the here and now; Chapters 5 and 6 move their sight and site to the messy details left out of utopian visions, such as untamable desire, wiliness, lazy men and fun-loving women, and all the practices we engage in that pose a threat to what is good and harmonious, or more importantly to our yearning for being part of the universe.

Chapter 1, 'Virtuous City: Sovereign, Courtier, Subject', maps the contours of the paradigmatic code of conduct befitting each member of an imagined ideal community visible in Solomon legends past and present. The ideal love relationship between 'man and woman', my update of the classical Chinese 'husband and wife', is overlaid with that of 'sovereign, courtier, and subject', my adaptation of the Chinese 'king and officer', to guide political authority and just rule. Love, coeval with reason, guides desire, a by-word for passion, to justice, to doing what is right, and to righting wrongs.

Chapter 2, 'Heroic Family: Love, Desire, Marriage', hones in on the role of the paradigmatic 'husband and wife' or 'man and woman' love in effecting harmony in the family, the microcosm of community in Harun al-Rashid myths.

Chapter 3, 'Harmonious Community: Fathers and Mothers, Sons and Daughters', looks at Solomon legends and Arabic epics, or romances, to tease out the ways in which adherence to the ideal 'man and woman' and 'parent and child' – my modernization of the Chinese 'father and son' relationships – in Arabic stories, and their transgression, lead respectively to the coherence and disintegration of both family and community.

Chapter 4, 'Alternative Society: The Fellowship of Men and Women', returns to the Harun al-Rashid legends and other stories modelled on them, and explores alternatives to the ideal community structured around sovereign, courtier, and subject when this community falls apart as a result of violations in its underpinning code of conduct. A 'sibling' relationship, or brotherhood in classical Chinese works, operates in concert with friendship to propose another form of ideal community that is similarly built around paradigmatic man-and-woman love.

The ethics of living for everyday come into focus in our contemplations of the relations between sovereign, courtier, and subject, parent and child, man and woman, siblings, friends, and the secular and divine. The paradigmatic sovereign–courtier–subject relationship underpins the structure of any political community based on justice, while the ideal parent and child, man-and-woman and sibling relationships offer a roadmap for the making of a harmonious society. Friendship expands the scope of society to include non-blood relations, and offers a corrective, where necessary, to corrupt rule and dysfunctional familial authority. The familial classical Chinese husband and wife, father and son, and brother and brother relationships in storytelling speak for the sovereign and courtier and friend and friend fellowships structuring the political elite. As such, these five relationships, particularly in their overlap, brought up to date in this book, become the cornerstones of the stories we tell about ourselves, metaphors for power and at the same time loci for the working out of ethics of living.

The earnestness of these chapters finds relief in Chapters 5 and 6. While Chapter 5, '*Joie de Vivre*: Life is a Banquet', reflects on, and even subverts, the stories we tell about our yearning for an ideal community, and challenges the idea of perfection our imagination conjures up, Chapter 6, 'Heaven on Earth: Storytelling and Meanings of Life', takes us further into a space where a different kind of impulse, such as spirituality, allows us to engage with life in a transcendental way. The relationship between the individual and the pleasures of life or the divine does not take the individual out of society; rather it affirms an individual's social role but at the same time provides a fresh lens on political and social strife. More importantly, this relationship points to lines of escape from political and social structures for individuals to pursue happiness while living meaningfully.

Chapter 1

Virtuous City: Sovereign, Courtier, Subject

> We certainly tested Solomon, reducing him to a mere skeleton on his throne.
>
> (Q. 38:34)

Solomon is prophet, king, wise judge, builder of temples, mosques and cities, and the supreme master of the universe ruling over a gargantuan dominion and over all living beings in the Abrahamic tradition. Even after his death, the treasures, magical beings and objects he has left behind continue to exert power on our imagination. Solomon's power emanates from his magical signet ring. It has the properties of both amulets and talismans. Solomon's ring gives whoever owns it absolute mastery over the universe. Its power is so alluring that all living beings covet it. Those tempered by wisdom gained from history know better than to own it or let it fall in the hands of those who desire it for the sake of power and domination.

We read a kindred story in J.R.R. Tolkien's *The Lord of the Rings*, which is one of the most famous political allegories of our time, thanks in large part to Peter Jackson's cinematic

Figure 4. Talismanic scroll bearing 'Solomon's seal'. Egypt, 11th century.

Figure 5. Seal ring from the late 15th to early 16th century, with inscribed verses known as the *Nad-i 'Ali*, an invocation to 'Ali ibn Abi Talib, son-in-law of the Prophet Muhammad.

adaptations. Inspired by biblical folklore and haunted by the two world wars of the twentieth century, *The Lord of the Rings* tells the story of an epic battle between good and evil centred around a magic ring. The forces of good, repres-ented by the fellowship of the ring, must first evade, then fight, the armies of evil seeking to possess the ring and use it to preside over Middle Earth. Ultimately, peace returns after many ferocious battles, but the journey is arduous. Members of the fellowship, led by Frodo and Aragorn, are tested to the limit and survive only if they curb their desire for the ring. Frodo is tempted again and again to keep the ring. And Aragorn goes through a journey of transformation that culminates in his becoming king.

The Lord of the Rings, like the Solomon legends in the *Thousand and One Nights*, is about the centrality of educating desire into love, in this case, desire for power into love for the greater good of humanity and communal harmony. Love, as we will see in the Solomon legends below, means faith in, and loyalty to, our fellow human beings. It is the cornerstone of social relationships and describes the conduct of all members of the ideal community, from the sovereign to his courtiers and subjects, in Solomon legends, in biblical folklore, *adab*, and Arabic storytelling.

The Code of Conduct for an Ideal Community

The exemplary sovereign in the Solomon legends is reincarnated in the first two cycles of stories that Shahrazad tells Shahriyar in the *Thousand and One Nights*: 'The Merchant and the Genie' and 'The Fisherman and the Demon', including the latter's framed story, 'The Enchanted King'. These tales form the core of the *Nights*, appearing in all editions, and their representation of worlds pervaded with chaos and requiring intervention mirrors the larger story in the *Nights*, in which Shahriyar discovers his wife's infidelity, kills her and seeks revenge by marrying a different woman every night only to kill her at dawn.

The stories that Shahrazad tells Shahriyar in 'The Merchant and the Genie' and 'The Fisherman and the Demon' offer a corrective. While the former story cycle revisits the marital infidelity Shahriyar experiences and shows its consequences in the break-up of social relationships, including the punishment he metes out on his subjects, the latter shows alternative courses of action for Shahriyar and for the men and women who belong to the community he oversees.

The events of these two stories take place in the aftermath of Solomon's death, in the magical world he has left behind, and they revive the legacy of his wise and just rule. The stories suggest a code of conduct for all members of the community, from the sovereign to his officers and subjects. In the way of stories, they do this by showing in a game of mirroring how any violation by any member can affect the community and destroy its harmony.

The Merchant and the Genie

'The Merchant and Genie' begins unremarkably, just like the *Nights*' frame story. An itinerant merchant sits down to a meal under a tree in an orchard. He eats dates and happily throws the stones left and right. Before he finishes, an angry

Figure 6. 'The Story of the Fisherman', by Duilio Cambellotti (1876–1960). Illustration for *The Arabian Nights*, c. 1912.

genie appears before him and demands his life as ransom for his son's life, for a stone carelessly thrown away by the merchant had accidentally killed the genie's child.

Similarly in the frame story, Shahriyar, King of Sasan, misses his brother Shahzaman, King of Samarkand, and sends for him. Shahzaman happily sets out to visit his brother. However, he returns to his palace unexpectedly to pick up a gift for his brother and sees his queen participating in an orgy with the palace slaves and slave-girls. He takes no action and leaves. At his brother's palace, he accidentally witnesses his brother's queen indulging in the same behaviour and he informs Shahriyar. Shahriyar kills his queen as well as her entourage in anger. He embarks on a journey of revenge and finally marries Shahrazad.

Shahrazad tells Shahriyar stories for one thousand and one nights, enabling him to see his experience in the context of the broader canvas of the complexity of human desire and he learns to love again. The stories Shahrazad tells him repeat, reflect, and refract Shahriyar's experience in such a way that shows him it is possible to recover from anger, to return to his benevolent and magnanimous rule, and to restore harmony to his family and community.

In 'The Merchant and the Genie' we hear stories of the break-up of two of our social relationships: those of 'husband and wife' and 'brother and brother'. The violations of the unspoken covenant binding these relationships cause the break-up of families and the exile of the protagonists. Three old men, travelling with a gazelle, two dogs, and a mule, respectively, come to the aid of the titular merchant condemned to death by the genie. Each tells the genie the story of the animals in their company.

The story told by the first old man shows betrayal of trust between husband and wife. The gazelle accompanying this man was in fact his first wife, but as she was barren he took a second wife, who gave him a son. In a jealous rage, while the man was away on a business trip, the first wife turned the second wife into a cow and her son into a calf. Upon his return, she tries to have him kill, with his own hand, the cow, the mother of his son, and the calf, his son, on Eid al-Adha, the Muslim Feast of Sacrifice. He looks into the eyes of the animals and hesitates. He delegates the task of slaughtering the cow to the shepherd, and gifts him the calf. The shepherd's daughter also knows magic and sees the human behind the animal façade. She restores the calf to his human form, marries him, and punishes the culprit.

The second story shifts our sight from marital problems to sibling rivalry. This old man explains that the dogs with him are his two brothers, and he tells the story of their trans-formation. The three brothers had inherited equal portions of their father's great fortune and, like him, went into trade. The storyteller succeeded but his brothers failed. They turned to him for help. He decided to go into business with them. He divided his gold dinars into two halves, hiding one portion, and splitting the other into three equal shares. He gave each of his two brothers one share and together they all embarked on a trade journey across the Indian Ocean. In one port city, the storyteller met a woman and married her. She joined their voyage, but after they set sail again, his two brothers jealously conspired to get rid of him. They crept into his cabin at night, wrapped him and his wife with the bed linen they were sleeping in, and threw them into the ocean. They did not know that their sister-in-law was a genie. She rescued herself and her husband and turned her brothers-in-law into dogs.

The third story resembles Shahriyar's story and returns our attention to the betrayal of trust between husband and wife. The third old man returns home from a long journey to find his wife in bed with a black slave. She turns her husband into a mule. He wanders in the streets until he reaches the butcher's shop. The butcher's daughter knows magic and, recognizing the human in him, turns him back into a man, and his wife into a mule.

Each story on its own ostensibly affirms and even magnifies the hurt, anger, and loss of faith Shahriyar felt upon witnessing his wife's infidelity, and implies that death was the only appropriate punishment for such a betrayal of trust. More importantly, the three stories seem to portray betrayal of trust as integral to human nature in general, and woman's character in particular, for which there could be no redemption.

Other elements, however, point to alternatives. The framing of the story and the second old man's story both show that some men and women can be trusted. The titular merchant – the one who threw the date stone – asks for a one-year respite from his punishment so he can go home and bid farewell to his family and friends. He does so and returns on time for his appointment with death. The second old man's wife is loyal. Each story's ending shows that death is not the only possible punishment for betrayal. The three old men do not abandon their responsibility as heads of their families, as well as their communities, but rather give up their vocation and spend the rest of their lives wandering the world with their transmogrified wives and brothers.

The Fisherman and the Demon

Personal tragedies take on communal proportions in the *Thousand and One Nights*, as we see in 'The Fisherman and the Demon'. The stories in this cycle pick up from where 'The Merchant and the Genie' leaves off, similarly mirroring and refracting the 'Shahriyar and Shahrazad' frame story. This time, they take us on a tour to another part of the Solomon legends, to the king's court and harem through the prism of a fisherman.

This story cycle also begins unremarkably. A humble fisherman habitually casts his net into the sea no more than four times a day. On an ill-omened morning, he catches in his net a dead donkey, a jug full of mud and sand, 'broken pots and pans, stones, bones, refuse, and the like', and finally 'a large long-necked brass jar, with a lead stopper bearing the mark of a seal ring'.[1] He opens the jar, and a demon whom Solomon had locked up in the jar for eight hundred years emerges, not to thank the fisherman for freeing him but to take his life. The fisherman tricks the demon back into the jar and seals it again. A conversation between the fisherman and the demon ensues, and the fisherman tells the demon a cycle of three frame-within-frame stories: 'King Yunan and the Sage Duban', 'The Husband and the Parrot,' and 'The King's Son and the She-Ghoul'.

These stories begin with a do-gooder, like the fisherman, who gets punished, not rewarded, for his good deed, but end with the punisher himself being punished. The parrot in 'The Husband and the Parrot' tells his master, a merchant, about the infidelity of his wife during his absence, only to be killed. The framing 'King Yunan and the Sage Duban' and the framed 'The King's Son and She-Ghoul' both show the havoc a jealous vizier can wreak in a king's family, but also show that such actions have consequences. The vizier who conspires to have the king's son killed by sending him to a she-ghoul is caught and punished. When King Yunan's vizier succeeds in turning the king against the sage Duban, the physician who had cured him of leprosy, Duban goes to meet his death, but before he is beheaded, he gives the king a poisoned book and the king dies too.

Having heard these three stories, the demon agrees not to kill the fisherman if the latter frees him again, and pledges to make him rich. He then takes the fisherman to a lake surrounded by four hills, telling him to take what he catches to the king of his city. In the lake are white, red, blue, and yellow fish. The fisherman catches one of each colour and takes them to the king. They naturally end up in the royal kitchen. But the fish are never cooked, and the king is thwarted from a coveted taste. As the pan heats up and the fish are thrown in, a genie or demon parts the kitchen wall and converses with the fish only to burn them to a crisp before disappearing through the crack in the wall again.

The king hears this and sets out for the lake where the fish originate. He scours the area and comes upon a great palace where he finds a young king whose lower half has been turned to stone. He was, he tells the older king in the inset story of 'The Enchanted King', betrayed by his queen, his cousin. She was a sorceress forced into the royal marriage but in love with a demon from the Qaf mountain. She drugged him every night then went to her lover. When he found out, he followed her to her love nest, where he struck the demon lover and left his wife untouched. His wife turned him into a half statue, his kingdom into a lake and his subjects, Christians, Jews, Muslims, and Zoroastrians, into the variously coloured fish in the lake. Life comes to a standstill in the community he rules. He looks over the lake in his half-statue state, and watches the only two living beings, his wife and her demon lover, betray him day and night.

The visiting king promises the enchanted king he will right the wrong. And he does. Like Shahriyar, he kills the demon lover. He then impersonates the demon, tricks the sorceress into breaking the spell, and kills her. However, unlike Shahriyar, he remembers to save the subjects, the living beings enchanted into fish. Normal life and harmony return but all is not the same. The saved kingdom is integrated into the saviour's kingdom. The young king follows the gallant older king home and remains there as a grateful boon companion. The vizier of his rescuer now rules his former kingdom.

This ending makes sense in accordance with the logic set up by a narrative that weaves into one two previously independent stories, 'The Fisherman and the Demon' and 'The Enchanted King'. These two stories, with the former framing the latter, are two sides of the same coin. The fisherman and the saviour king live on and conduct themselves according to love, here, a metaphor for the contract that binds the king, his officers, and their subjects. The demon and the queen are parallels that accentuate the contrasts between the fisherman and the demon, the saviour king and the enchanted king, the enchanted king and the demon lover, and the demon and the demon lover. Their conduct, driven by desire gone awry, breaks up families, and tears communities asunder. Together, the framing story of 'The Fisherman and the Demon' and the framed story of 'The Enchanted King' show the ways in which an ideal community survives and thrives on love, and on educating the desire of every member into love. In this labyrinth of narrative intersections, the fisherman is the nexus on which the seemingly disparate strands hang.

Ideal Kingship and its Qualities

The fisherman is the representative of the king and kingship. He is a model citizen who embodies *'aql* (reason) and *'adl* (justice), the key principles of an ideal kingship overseen and maintained by the king, whose authority and legitimacy are derived from faith, symbolized in this cycle by Solomon, as well as from his conduct. Love in this context denotes not only proper desire informed by reason but also its resultant justice. The fisherman has a clear advantage over the demon. The demon, after all, was banished to the bottom of the sea for refusing to obey Solomon. Obedience, in this context, is not paying lip service to the authority of Solomon but abiding by a code of conduct that would ensure individual salvation and communal harmony.

The demon learns this vital lesson from the fisherman. He exits the bottle in exuberance, thinking that in the aftermath of Solomon's death he can do as he wishes and no longer has

Figure 7. 'Genie of the Lamp', by Edmund Dulac (1882–1953). Illustration from *Sinbad the Sailor & Other Stories from the Arabian Nights*.

to fear Solomon's power or obey his edicts. But this is not how the world works. The demon is outwitted by the fisherman and ends up back in the bottle until he promises to observe one simple principle: not to punish the one who has done him good, a contextualized summation of *'adl* based on rewarding the good and righting the wrong. The cycle of stories the fisherman tells the demon, 'King Yunan and the Sage Duban', and the resolution of 'The Enchanted King' reinforce this.

Things go terribly wrong for King Yunan when he decides to cut off Duban's head: he 'insisted on destroying the sage, and Almighty God destroyed him'.[2] In punishing good with evil, Yunan breached the unwritten contract of kingship and precipitated the ruin of his kingdom. The lines of poetry recited by Duban's severed head as it watches Yunan die of Duban's poison are instructive:

> For long they ruled us arbitrarily,
> But suddenly vanished their powerful rule.
> Had they been just, they would have
>   happily
> Lived, but they oppressed, and punishing
>   fate
> Afflicted them with ruin deservedly,
> And on the morrow the world taunted them,
> "'Tis tit for tat; blame not just destiny."[3]

Here, the fate of rule, or more aptly kingship, is upheld by its adherence to justice, and when rule turns to oppression, only affliction and ruin lie ahead. Destiny is not random but is determined by actions taken. As the fisherman puts it to the demon, "I did you a good turn, and you are about to repay me with a bad one." The demon learns from 'Yunan and Duban' that his intent to harm will have dire consequences. Here, the driver of the action becomes crucial in restraining the demon's will, therefore, shaping the fisherman's destiny.

The fisherman outwits the demon not only because he is cleverer but also because his actions are driven by ʿaql. At the critical moment, when the fisherman realizes that reasoning with the demon will not lead to his salvation and resorts to tricking the demon back into the bottle, he reminds himself that, "He is only a demon, while I am a human being, whom God has endowed with reason [and thereby made superior to him]. He may use demonic wiles on me, but I will use my reason to deal with him."[4] The reference to ʿaql here is parallel to that made by Duban, also at a critical moment, when he realizes that Yunan will not spare his life. Weeping, Duban cites these lines seemingly to mock his own naïveté:

> Maymuna is deprived of the marks of
>   reason,
> Even though her father was descended from
>   a line of sages.
> He never walked on land or settled
>   anywhere,
> Unless guided by its light, and avoided slip-
>   ping he did.[5]

There is a double-entendre here. It refers to both his own folly – how could he have been so foolish as to think his good deed would be rewarded not punished – and to the king's foolishness, his slip in reason, an English approximation of *'aql*.

'Aql

In Arabic, the term *'aql* has a set of connotations, referents and associations pervasive in pre-modern Arabic writing of all kinds that are deeply rooted in Arabic–Islamic worldview, heir to the region's ancient civilizations. *'Aql*, and its attendant qualities, in fact, form the kernel around which kingship and community are envisioned and constructed.

'Aql in *Lisan al-'arab*, one of the most authoritative lexicons in Arabic, compiled by Ibn Manzur (d. 1312), is the human ability to curb an action. Ibn al-Jawzi (d. 1200) describes *'aql* as the discernment of what is possible and what is impossible; and the suppression of desires requiring instant gratification (but granting only temporary pleasure). It is humankind's path to the knowledge of God and His prophets and to the realization of the importance of following their commands. It enables them to assess situations and anticipate the consequences of actions taken and thereby to act without jeopardizing their own interest. It empowers them to make use of other living beings (including animals) and put them to their service. It encourages virtues and deters vices, buttresses resolutions and strengthens determinations, and brings about good and banishes evil.

Figure 8. Mirror interpreted as showing Solomon and his demons. Front shows the Throne Verse, Q. 2:255.

In his view of the role of ʿaql in individual and communal life, Ibn al-Jawzi was heir to a long tradition of discourses on community and, more particularly, leadership of this community. His view echoes what is already found in *adab* and in philosophical writings, where ʿaql and ʿadl, reason and justice, are always inextricably linked.[6]

In *adab*, Ibn al-Muqaffaʿ (d. ca. 757) had already expounded on the communal role of

ʿaql through the voice of Bidpai in *Kalila wa Dimna*, his translation from Persian of a collection of Indian animal stories.[7] This seminal work finds reverberations in all later works of the genre known as the 'mirror for princes' intended to provide instructions for the sovereign and his officers on the protocols of just rule in a kingdom. *ʿAql* and *ʿadl* are two qualities required in a king together with *hikma* and uprightness (*ʿiffa*). Whereas *ʿaql* denotes forbearance, patience and endurance, and sobriety and dignity, and *ʿadl* denotes truthfulness, doing good, proper conduct, and the observation of actions and their consequences on and of self and others, *hikma* encompasses knowledge, culture (*adab*), and deliberation; and *ʿiffa* modesty, generosity, the upkeep of honour, and pride.

Al-Farabi (d. 950) similarly identifies justice as one of the qualities required in the leader of a community, whom he calls an imam, linking it to abilities associated with *ʿaql* in his philosophical treatise on 'The Perfect State' (*al-madina al-fadila*). The ideal citizen, the *ʿaqil*, is good at understanding, well provided with ready intelligence, and fond of learning and acquiring knowledge. He loves truth and truthful men and hates falsehood and liars. He values generosity and honour, his soul rising above everything that is ugly and base, to loftier things, justice (*ʿadl*), and just people. Justice entails hating oppression and injustice and those who practise them; giving himself and others their due; urging people to act justly and showing pity to those who are oppressed by injustice; and lending support to what he considers to be beautiful and noble and just. He is also strong and forthright.

For al-Farabi, ʿaql presides over an ideal community giving structure to learning and knowledge, culture and proper conduct, all of which serve as a framework for maintaining and administering justice. Justice is most visible in the manifestation of the principles of 'rewarding good and punishing evil' and 'righting wrong' that lie at the heart of the story of the 'Fisherman and the Demon'. When these principles are upset, this is an indication that reason, as a driving force and paradigm, has been violated, and harmony has turned into chaos.

Hawa

The opposite of ʿaql in the great Arabic dictionary, Lisan al-ʿArab, is humq. According to Ibn al-Jawzi, humq (or hamaqa) denotes stagnation and wasted effort. It also means using the wrong means to achieve a sound end. It is not the only antonym of ʿaql. Al-Farabi juxtaposes his virtuous city, al-madina al-fadila, to other cities whose people follow the paths of ignorance, sin, distortion, and lack of guidance. The residents of these cities follow worldly pursuits and seek the immediate gratification of their needs and desires. It is no wonder, then, that al-Farabi stipulates that the leader of his perfect state 'should by nature not crave for food and drink and sexual intercourse and [should] have a natural aversion to gambling and hatred of the pleasures which these pursuits provide,' and that 'Dirham and dinar and other worldly pursuits should be of little value in his view.'[8] The items named here, food, drink, money, and sex, are all objects of desire that, when they become an obsession, can disrupt and disable the workings of reason.

Ibn al-Jawzi calls this type of excess *hawa*. This term denotes emotions ranging from simple first inclination to love, passion, and obsession, that lead to, and are driven by, desire (*shahwa*). But *hawa* is condemned only when it exceeds the boundaries of an initial inclination and develops into a full-fledged desire, or will, that gives immediate pleasure but necessarily ends in pain or ruin, when it arrests *'aql*'s ability to keep one's desires reined in.

Figure 9. 'The Fisherman and the Genie', by Edmund Dulac (1882–1953).

When *hawa* overwhelms ʿ*aql*, the world is turned upside down. The initial encounter between the juxtaposed fisherman and the demon facilitates and brings about another set of encounter and juxtaposition, that of the saviour king and the enchanted king. The saviour king, like the fisherman, is an epitome of ʿ*aql*. He is attentive to the goings-on in his kingdom and once he discovers the story of the enchanted king he acts swiftly to 'right the wrong'. His astute observance of ʿ*aql* brings him well-deserved reward – he expands his kingdom into an empire. The enchanted king, though saved, must give up his kingdom to the saviour king's vizier and serve his saviour as courtier. But what is the colossal wrong that can only be redeemed with the loss of a kingdom?

The contrast between the kingdom ruled by the older king and that by his younger counter-part provides a clue. There is no unhealthy desire in the older king, who lives by the rules of the symbolic order overseen by ʿ*aql* and makes sure that it pervades his kingdom. His conduct bespeaks the qualities of a king as stipulated by Ibn al-Muqaffaʿ and of a leader of the virtuous city as described by al-Farabi. His appetite for a tantalizing dish to be made from the colourful fish is tempered by a stateliness conveyed in Ibn al-Muqaffaʿ's ʿ*aql*, *hikma*, ʿ*iffa* and ʿ*adl*. When he is deprived of an eagerly anticipated delicacy, he does not chop off anyone's head; rather, he embarks on an investigative journey that will lead to discovering an injustice in need of redress.

ʿAql and Hawa

The older king's justice is swift, and he does as al-Farabi would have the leader of his 'perfect state' do and acts decisively, ridding the enchanted kingdom of the queen and her demon lover. Such a king, unsurprisingly in an ideal world, has the loyalty of his officers and obedience of his subjects. His vizier safeguards his kingdom on his behalf while he is away for a year, and the fisherman upholds the paradigmatic code of conduct. That the fisherman succeeds in domesticating the demon and the sea world is a clear clue to the state of harmony that permeates the kingdom of which he is citizen.

The 'enchanted kingdom' contrarily falls under the spell of desire. The queen and her demon lover in the 'Enchanted King' are, like the demon in 'The Fisherman and the Demon', driven by their unruly *hawa*. Their actions, determined by their desire (*shahwa*) for each other, lead to indiscretion, provoke a reaction from the king, and condemn the kingdom to a sub-human mode of existence.

There is, however, something un-Shahriyar-like in the young king's reaction that distinguishes him from his saviour. Like Shahriyar, the king thinks he is happily married (to his cousin) until he discovers his wife's betrayal. Unlike Shahriyar, who kills the adulterers in a swift, decisive action, this king fails to rectify the situation. Upon hearing the murmurs of his maids, he follows his wife and spies her in action with her demon lover. He rushes to kill his rival and wounds him, then hurries to leave without making certain of the demon's death. More poignantly, he does not attempt to punish his wife. When he spares his wife, his kingdom falls prey to black magic: he loses half of his humanity, his kingdom turns into a sea and his subjects into fish. For, unlike the fisherman who curbs the demon's *hawa*, he fails to rule both – desire in himself and his kingdom. He himself is subject to *hawa*, as the love poems he recites show, and lets his queen, desire, take over.

There is no redemption for an un-Shahriyar-like king. He may be saved but he loses his entitlement to the crown. But Shahriyar himself falls short of the ideal king, for unlike the saviour king in 'The Fisherman and Demon', he punishes evil for his own gratification and forgets to consider the consequences of his action on the harmony in the community he rules. No king under the influence of *hawa*, not even Solomon, as we shall see, can administer justice – rewarding the right and punishing the wrong – when he is not in enough possession of *'aql* to control his desire. The contrast between the enchanted kingdom and its former incarnation and, more particularly, the other kingdom, accentuated by the parallel roles of the demons and the queen in the stories, brings to the fore the dialectics between reason and passion in the *Nights*.

'The Fisherman and the Demon' is a morality tale in the vein of the 'mirror for princes' genre. The interplay between reason and passion, or love and desire, takes centre-stage in a play intended to teach both ruler and ruled the proper rites of political authority that must be guided by a workable system of justice.

There are two discourses on community embedded in these stories. The discourse on proper love frames another discourse on an ideal community. Reason ensures communal harmony and passion leads to chaos. The ideal community is the world in which royal love is proper, and its opposite is a world ruled by improper desire. Legitimate kingship in these stories is not only the conclusion of a proper royal love match, but also an appropriate code of conduct. The prosperity of kingship rests additionally on the king's ability to manage desires of all kinds in his kingdom. As we see in 'The Fisherman and the Demon', the king must personify reason and dispense justice accordingly, rewarding the good, punishing the bad, and righting the wrong. The king's authority is only legitimate and oper-ative when desire is transformed by reason into proper conduct, into love.

The overall happy ending sees the two kings marrying the two daughters of the fisherman. This may seem gratuitous at first reading, but on second thought it manifests itself as a sensible conclusion to the narrative strands around king-ship and community. Marriage in this context is a metaphor for the contract that binds the king to his officers, subjects and, above all, kingship and kingdom. It is a contract based on reason that ensures harmony, prosperity, and continuity of the kingdom of the story. Love is the commit-ment, not only of a king to a queen, but also of kingship to reason.

Love (*hubb* or *mahabba*), as Arabic theories of love tell us, may be founded on reason; in fact, the best kind is among the *ʿaqilun* – between king and vizier, friend and friend, or man and

Figure 10. 'The Fisherman and the Afrite (or Genie), designed by John La Farge (1835–1910). Engraved by Henry Marsh (1826–1912).

woman. When in charge, reason stops love from turning into the kind of excessive passion (*'ishq*), that results in madness or mortal peril. 'The Fisherman and the Demon' gives a glimpse of the workings of the triad of power, justice and reason in an ideal community following a bottom-up trajectory. The king, his vizier, and the fisherman are manifestations of the same code of conduct appropriate to an ideal community.[9]

Stories as Guidelines for Conduct

Let us return briefly to *The Lord of the Rings*. The tension in the Arabic Solomon legends between desire and love, passion and reason serves as the axis around which individual entitlement and responsibility, and communal order and disorder, are worked out. Such lessons for our conduct, such as greed and modesty, right and wrong, justice and tyranny, find reverberations in Tolkien's political allegory. Just as we see the fisherman in Frodo, in fact, in all the hobbits, we see the good king in Aragorn. Even his love story with Arwen, an elf, echoes the perfect love we find between the king and queen of an ideal kingdom in the *Nights*.

Members of the fellowship of the ring follow the path of reason, and Sauron and his lackeys pursue passion in three ways: Gollum desires the ring for its own sake, a sensation Frodo shares but resists; Saruman, wizard and antithesis of Gandalf, craves absolute power and total domination; and the orcs or goblins give in to Sauron's tyranny and promise of power, and thrive on violence and disorder. The paradigmatic code of conduct structured around love that underpins 'sovereign, courtier and subject,' 'man-and-woman', and here also 'friends', of which we will see more in Chapter 4, remains operative here. Any violation of this code of conduct puts the community at risk. Even Solomon is not immune to losing his power and kingship. We see this play out in the accounts of his loss of his signet ring in the tales of the prophets (*qisas al-anbiya*) found in both history and Qur'anic exegesis.[10]

This episode appears at the end of the accounts of Solomon's life, often preceding the final episode on his death. It is offered as an explanation of Q. 38:34, quoted at the beginning of this chapter, which refers to a body being placed on the throne in Solomon's stead. In an uncanny way, this story crystallizes Solomon's persona. It recounts his conquest of an island in the sea ruled by Saydun, his capture of Saydun's daughter, Jarada, and her unhappiness in his harem. As the story unfolds, Jarada asks Solomon to have his genies build an effigy of her father. Out of love, Solomon acquiesces. Jarada then dresses the effigy with her father's clothes and worships him for 40 days behind Solomon's back. Asaf b. Barkhiya, Solomon's scribe, discovers this and tells Solomon that 'Someone other than God has been worshipped in your house for 40 days, because of the whim of a woman.'[11] Solomon destroys the idol, punishes Jarada and her slave-girls, and then puts on 'garments of purification, woven by virgins',[12] and goes out into the desert and penitently begs God for forgiveness for one entire day. He then returns to his home.

Entering, he leaves his ring with his faithful woman servant, al-Amina. Sakhr, the demon who was master of the sea, comes to her in the likeness of Solomon and claims the ring. When the real Solomon, now completely altered and unrecognizable, returns to claim his ring, al-Amina does not know him and tells him that Solomon has already taken his ring. Renounced by his people, Solomon departs to the sea. There he works as a labourer in the fish market for 40 days. When Sakhr realizes that Asaf b. Barkhiya suspects him, he runs away and throws the ring into the sea. It happens to be swallowed by the one fish Solomon keeps for his dinner. As he slits open the fish to clean it, he finds the ring and is able to recover his kingdom. Solomon then has Sakhr sealed in a bottle and thrown into the sea.

This is the plot of the story of Solomon's ring in the various histories in the Abrahamic tradition. The Jewish and Muslim versions have in common Solomon's love for women. The difference is that in the Jewish version this episode marks the beginning of his end as king for marrying an outsider, but in the Arabic version it represents a temporary lapse, or distraction (*fitna* in Arabic), and is, moreover, transformed into an exemplar of the repentance of an unintended 'sinner' (here, a prophet-king), of God's boundless forgiveness and, above all, of His justice. Solomon's carnal desire serves as the catalyst for expressions of piety in history, exegesis, or storytelling. None deviates from the above narrative of Solomon's exile structured around Jarada and her idolatry. The story is a warning against allowing idolatry to be committed unwittingly, as Jarada does in Solomon's home. It is always better to be overcautious than lackadaisical.

Intention too is critical in how an accidental offender is punished. There are no details of Jarada's punishment, but Solomon's punishments are most elaborate. The symmetry in how 'sin' and 'punishment' are aligned gives a sense of the imagined ideal justice. The punishment for 40 days of unintended idolatry is 40 days of exile from power, community, and home. Wholehearted repentance and uninterrupted prayer and fasting for an entire day are not enough. The physical symptoms of Solomon's exile – his complete change of appearance, his wandering, his suffering at the hands of his own subjects, and Sakhr's violation of his wives – bring an abstract idea floating in lofty clouds down to earth, driving the message home in concrete terms. What happens in the privacy of a king's home, between husband and wife, as we shall see in the next chapter on the Harun al-Rashid myths, has an impact not only on family but also on community.

Chapter 2

Heroic Family: Love, Desire, Marriage

'Loyalty is beautiful, and treachery is ugly.'
    'Aziza, 'The story of 'Aziz and 'Aziza'

Like Solomon, Harun al-Rashid has inspired storytellers since the eighth century. The latter's portrayals in both Arabic and Orientalist historical and literary writings have understandably been subject to continuous scrutiny, each in turn producing a new icon based on but departing from previous ones. While some, such as the contemporary French historian André Clot, have sought to portray the complexity of his rule, others, such as American artist and writer Milton Klonsky, have portrayed him as the epitome of tyranny.[1]

In recent Arabic scholarship on Harun al-Rashid, there have been many attempts to rehabilitate his image and rescue his reputation from tyranny and moral corruption. Although Ahmad Amin (d. 1954) presents Harun al-Rashid in all his multifaceted splendour, and Muhammad 'Abd al-Rahman Yunus daringly relates political tyranny to sexual debauchery in stories structured around him,[2] scholars intolerant of ambiguity, and going against the grain of medieval Arabic-Islamic culture, feel they must rise to his defence and restore his reputation as not only a just ruler, but also a pious Muslim who observed the strict rules of Islam. Such scholars remove any mention of his abuse of power, and his concubines and drinking parties from his life and rule, harem and court, and offer us a biography of a devout Muslim who ruled justly, wisely and magnanimously.[3] Stories about his wisdom, generosity, appreciation of wise counsel, readiness to forgive, and decisiveness in rule and warfare are magnified, but anecdotes about his conduct as ruler at court in the pre-modern *adab* tradition and the stories about his nocturnal adventures in the *Nights* are expunged from these accounts.

Such a cleansing operation, however, tells us more about Harun al-Rashid's powerful presence in the Arabic cultural and literary imaginary as head of both family and community. The ways in which representations of his court and harem are tinkered with, edited, and transformed give us a sense of the importance of Harun al-Rashid's symbolic value for generations of Arabs and Muslims.

In the *Nights*, stories centred around Harun al-Rashid are framed by an ideology of monogamy, in which the love that structures a husband-and-wife or man-and-woman relationship plays a key role in the fate of the community. This is evident even in the more liberal representations of his character and rule. Two television adaptations may suffice as examples:

Figure 11. 'Haroun al-Raschid', by Julius Köckert (1827–1918). An orientalist illustration used in an edition of the *Thousand and One Nights*.

the prize-winning Egyptian production, *Harun al-Rashid* (1997), and the Syrian production, also called *Harun al-Rashid* (2018). Both were produced for the Ramadan season and are pious. However, they do not shy away from the complexity of Harun al-Rashid's political career and social life but rather combine these to make statements about the style and quality of his conduct and leadership.

In the former, the Egyptian actor Nur al-Sharif (d. 2015) portrays Harun al-Rashid as a Sufi who, albeit fully cognizant of his responsibility as the leader of the Muslim community, thirsts for a peaceful life spent away from court intrigues and harem politics but in remembrance of God and the companionship of a pious and wise woman. In the Syrian production, Qusay

Khuli's Harun al-Rashid is a skillful politician who successfully manages the competing claims made on him by the members of both his court and harem and strikes a delicate balance among the various players in the games of power unfolding before him. He ensures stability, peace, and justice in his domain.

Harun al-Rashid, unsurprisingly, is Shahriyar even in contemporary imaginings. For example, the Egyptian television series that re-wrote the *Thousand and One Nights* for the 1984 Ramadan season has Shahrazad travel through time from modern Cairo to Shahriyar's kingdom, located in time immemorial, where she treats him and heals him from his narcissism and tyranny. Chiding him as a dictator, Shahrazad works to instill in Shahriyar ideas of gender equality as well as democracy.

In this re-telling of the Harun al-Rashid stories, Najla' Fathi and Husayn Fahmi, who play Shahrazad and Shahriyar, also impersonate, for example, Zubayda and Harun al-Rashid, thus overlapping the patterns of Shahriyar's power with those of Harun al-Rashid. They also play merchants, working class characters, and slaves – here Najla' Fathi embodies the erudite concubine figure in the *Nights* and pre-modern Arabic writings – and together, they take us on a journey of educating passion into love, tyranny into justice, and dictatorship into democracy. In this story of the education of the king and kingship, power and sex are inseparable, and the love between man and woman, or the husband-and-wife relationship in Chinese, is the hero. In the *Nights'* Harun al-Rashid stories, the ideology of monogamy weaves historical information and *adab* anecdotes into fictional tales of wonder and marvel in which harem and court are overlapped, and polity, society and family are collapsed into one.

Family is Community

The Harun al-Rashid stories in the *Nights* could have easily been lifted out of *Kitab al-Aghani*, which Abu'l-Faraj al-Isfahani (d. 967) compiled at the behest of Harun al-Rashid around the hundred tunes or melodies (*sawt*). These resonate with the famous Arabic love stories, epitomized by the Layla and Majnun legends,

Figure 12. 'Laila and Majnun', performed at the opening ceremony for the 2015 European Games in Baku Olympic Stadium June 13, 2015 in Baku, Azerbaijan.

brought into one compilation, and genre, by al-Sarraj (d. 1106) under the title *Martyrs of Love* (*Masari' al-'ushshaq*). 'The story of Anis al-Jalis and Nur al-Din b. Khaqan', for example, smacks of a tale that al-Sarraj relates about Harun al-Rashid and an unnamed slave-girl who refused to be sold even to the caliph himself after her master's death. In the end, Harun al-Rashid bought her, freed her and gave her an income as a reward not only for her devotion to her original master but also for her hapless master's love for her. 'The Story of Nur al-Din 'Ali b. Bakkar and Shams al-Nahar', another Harun al-Rashid story, echoes the Layla and Majnun legends.

Layla and Majnun's choice to devote themselves exclusively to each other creates a stark contrast to the lifestyle led by Harun al-Rashid and his concubines. The phrase Harun al-Rashid and his slave-girls (*Harun al-Rashid wa jawarihi*) in Arabic today conjures up the life of wine, music, and pleasure in Harun al-Rashid's court and harem as evoked in the *Kitab al-Aghani*. It both pokes fun at, and frowns upon, the excess associated with his lifestyle. More importantly, it denounces sexual excess as an expression of male power, and of tyranny.

The Harun al-Rashid stories in the *Nights* construct an ideal community in the dialogue they stage between the *Nights* and *adab*. They play with the stories of martyrs of love, bringing their inherent ideology of monogamy into stories of harem politics and court intrigues in the *Kitab*

Figure 13. Majnun in the Wilderness. Folio from a manuscript of the *Collected Works* (*Divan*) of Sultan Ibrahim Mirza (fol. 36).

al-aghani. The husband-and-wife relationship is overlaid with a sovereign-courtier-and-subject relationship in the way the tales in the *Nights* play with stories and genres, with writing and reading, and with telling and listening.

The stories told about and in the harem are linked to other stories told about and at court. In 'The Porter and Three Ladies of Baghdad', the three *qalandar*s, or itinerant Sufis, tell their stories in the harem at night but the two ladies tell theirs at court the next morning. Harun al-Rashid holds court more like a patron of an *adab* salon in the *Kitab al-Aghani* than a commander of the faithful who leads prayers, goes on pilgrimage, conducts military campaigns, and manages complex political and financial relations. The events in ''Ali b. Bakkar and Shams al-Nahar', for example, are structured around love poems, or songs, uttered and at times exchanged between the two lovers.

The stories begin with Harun al-Rashid's nocturnal journeys in Baghdad. Harun al-Rashid is a benevolent tyrant who, like 'Umar b. al-Khattab, the second of the Guided Caliphs, lives amongst his people rather than in an ivory tower. After a busy day at court, he often forsakes the pleasures of his harem, and goes out to the streets to inspect the affairs of his dominion in person, to mingle with those he rules, and to listen to what they have to say before he dispenses justice. His mobile cabinet is an entourage of three: himself, his vizier Ja'far (al-Barmaki), and his bodyguard Masrur. Together they disguise themselves as merchants and wander the streets of Baghdad at night.

The stories of injustice that unfold before Harun al-Rashid are variations on the same theme, akin to those discussed in Chapter 1: love unrequited or betrayed leads to tragedy or crime. He then intervenes to right wrongs, punishing the wrong doers and rewarding those who do good, and bestowing happiness on all. Justice is not only righting wrongs, as we saw in Chapter 1, but also showing mercy and compensating for wrongs, as we will see respectively in 'The Three Apples' and 'The Porter and the Three Ladies of Baghdad'. Justice may follow a simple formula, but it is nevertheless Harun al-Rashid's responsibility towards the community under his care. He may not be Solomon, but he feels equally accountable to God. His vizier, Ja'far, like his counterparts in Solomon legends, shares this burden of rule.

The Three Apples

When Harun al-Rashid sees the dismembered body of a murder victim in 'The Three Apples', and notes 'that the girl had been cut into nineteen pieces', he 'felt sad and sorry for her' and 'turned to Ja'far angrily, "You dog of a vizier, people are being killed and thrown into the river in my city, while I bear the responsibility till Doomsday."'[4] Ja'far may not be proactive in 'find[ing] her killer', choosing to wait for God's mercy, but he never for a minute considers offering up even a criminal in Baghdad's prison to save his own neck. Harun al-Rashid does not solve the murder, but orders Ja'far to do so, 'If you do not find me her killer, I will hang you and hang forty of your kinsmen with you.'[5] The details of the murder, revealed from the perspective of hindsight, will make his threat unnecessary and change the course of his action.

This crime-of-passion story comprises a series of coincidences. It begins with a merchant buying three apples from the orchards of Harun al-Rashid in Basra for his ill wife. Seeing one of the apples in the hands of a black slave in the street and that one of the three apples is missing from the three he bought for his wife, he becomes jealous, kills his wife, cuts her up, and throws her body parts in the Tigris. The resolution unfolds through a similar series of coincidences. Jaʿfar sees a Basran apple in the hand of his young daughter, inquires and finds out that one of his black slaves snatched the apple from the young son of the murderer who in turn stole it from the three apples his father bought for his mother.

In response to Harun al-Rashid's incredulity, Jaʿfar tells him the story of 'The Two Viziers, Nur al-Din ʿAli al-Misri and Badr al-Din al-Basri', in which the enduring love between the daughter and son of the estranged brothers, the two viziers, guides the family reunion that takes place at the end of the story (discussed further in Chapter 4). Moved by the story, Harun al-Rashid abandons his intention to 'avenge this girl and put her murderer to the worst of deaths';[6] instead he lets Jaʿfar's black slave go and, like the king in 'The Fisherman and the Demon', he 'gave the young man one of his choice concubines, settled him on a sufficient income, and made him one of his companions to the end of his days'.[7]

The Porter and the Three Ladies of Baghdad
Here, Harun al-Rashid chances upon the house of the three ladies on another of his nocturnal journeys, and sees cruelty unfold before his eyes when the mistress of the house beats her two dogs, and her companion flogs herself. Incensed, he demands an explanation, which triggers the wrath of the mistress of the house who threatens to punish them. The three *qalandar*s seeking shelter that night volunteer to tell their stories to save Harun al-Rashid and his entourage. Harun al-Rashid then reveals himself and has everyone present that night brought to his court in the morning. He now hears the ladies' stories.

When he hears that the three *qalandar*s are in fact sons of kings who, betrayed by their fathers' brother or viziers, lost everything; that the mistress of the house was a rich merchant who lost her husband due to her two sisters' envy; and that her companion was cast out by her husband due to the mischief of a jealous party, he goes to work on righting the wrongs done to his subjects. He first has the sisters of the mistress of the house, who had been transformed into dogs as punishment for their betrayal, restored to their human form. He then plays the matchmaker and marries the three *qalandar*s to the three sisters. Finally, he receives intelligence that the second lady's husband is in fact his son, al-Amin, and he effects a reconciliation.

Harun al-Rashid is pragmatic and merciful in righting wrongs. The black slave in 'The Three

Apples' may be the catalyst for murder, but he did not steal the apple with the intent to kill or cause harm and his death will not right the wrong done. The young man who killed his wife out of jealousy and pride is remorseful, and his father-in-law is willing to ransom his son-in-law with his own life rather than to seek ransom for his murdered daughter. Ja'far may be useless as a detective, but his patience and endurance allow for the facts to unfold naturally. What purpose would their punishment serve?

Similarly, the kingdoms that the three *qalandar*s ought to have inherited in 'The Porter and the Three Ladies of Baghdad', like that of the enchanted king in 'The Fisherman and the Demon', have disintegrated. The three sisters have suffered enough. Rather than causing more pain, Harun al-Rashid creates new families, hoping that under his care, these families will eventually cohere. For family is the microcosm of community, and its cohesion is the foundation of communal harmony. This may not be justice as we understand it today, but the impulse to focus on the present and the living, and to let go of the past and its trespasses can find sympathy with us.

The insertion of the story of al-Amin's concubine, the story of the second lady in 'The Porter and the Three Ladies of Baghdad', anticipates two 'martyrs of love' stories: '´Ali b. Bakkar and Shams al-Nahar' and 'Anis al-Jalis and Nur al-Din'. The story of the second lady in 'The Porter and the Three Ladies of Baghdad' recounts

how a favourite of al-Amin falls foul of a practical joke and subsequent malicious rumours
– she is bitten on the lip by a strange young man
she encounters on a shopping trip only to have
jealous concubines spread rumours of her infidelity – and she is first banished by al-Amin and
later redeemed by Harun al-Rashid. The 'martyrs
of love' stories demonstrate that both family and
community necessarily cohere around love and
loyalty, or more aptly, loyalty in love.

ʿAli b. Bakkar and Shams al-Nahar

Harun al-Rashid, like Solomon before him and
al-Amin, his son, after him, need not abide by the
ideology of monogamy himself, but as a good
caliph he ensures that its inherent code of conduct
is supported and upheld in the community he
rules. In "ʿAli b. Bakkar and Shams al-Nahar,' he
even privileges benevolence over his own pride.
ʿAli b. Bakkar, the descendant of a Persian royal
family, conducts a love affair with one of Harun
al-Rashid's favourite concubines, Shams al-Nahar,
right under his nose. He meets Shams al-Nahar in
the shop of a perfumer and they manage to meet
in person twice, once in her private chambers in
the harem, and the other time in the home of the
jeweller, but they are interrupted on both occasions. Fear hovers in the air and they conduct
their love affair secretly through exchange of
news, messages, and poems delivered by their
go-betweens. The protagonists die, and on the
same day too, as one would find in the stories of
Masariʿ al-ʿushshaq. Their friends bury them next

Figure 14. Manuscripts of *Mi'a layla wa layla* and *Kitab al-Jaghrafiya* (*One Hundred and One Nights* and the *Book of Geography*). This manuscript contains the earliest extant copy of al-Zuhri's *Book of Geography*, followed by one of the earliest versions of the famous stories of the Abbasid caliph Harun al-Rashid, *A Thousand and One Nights*, thought to have been adapted from a Persian source.

to each other. Harun al-Rashid hears murmurs of the affair but chooses not to investigate.

Anis al-Jalis and Nur al-Din b. Khaqan

Harun al-Rashid takes an active role in rewarding loyalty in love in 'Anis al-Jalis and Nur al-Din b. Khaqan.' The good king of Basra,[8] Muhammad b. Sulayman al-Zaynabi, has a good vizier and a bad vizier. The good vizier, Fadl al-Din b. Khaqan, purchases a slave-girl, Anis al-Jalis, for the king and at his request, for 1,000 gold dinars. Anis al-Jalis meets Nur al-Din, Fadl al-Din's philandering son, and they fall in love. Fadl al-Din orders Nur al-Din to marry Anis al-Jalis and more importantly never to take another wife or concubine or resell Anis al-Jalis. He soon dies and Nur al-Din squanders all his inheritance. His friends turn away from him, even those who received gifts and help from him. He contemplates selling Anis al-Jalis at the slave market and has an altercation with al-Mu'in b. Sawi, the evil vizier. As al-Mu'in b. Sawi comes after him, Nur al-Din runs away, taking with him Anis al-Jalis, from whom he cannot be parted. Arriving in Baghdad, they squat in one of Harun al-Rashid's palaces. They even make themselves at home and stage song and dance parties.

When Harun al-Rashid hears noise from afar and goes to investigate, this time disguised as a fisherman, he finds out about the injustice behind the lovers' exile. Harun al-Rashid springs into action. He sends Nur al-Din home with a letter to the king of Basra for him to remove al-Mu'in b. Sawi as vizier and appoint Nur al-Din in his instead. He even sends Ja'far to make sure all is in order, just like the king in 'The Fisherman and the Demon'. Indeed, al-Mu'in b. Sawi plots to have Nur al-Din killed but Ja'far arrives in time to save the day. He takes Nur al-Din back to Baghdad. Harun al-Rashid frees Anis al-Jalis and gifts her to him, appointing them both his boon companions.

Love and Loyalty

Love is not just love here; rather, love and loyalty are the mechanism for discovering injustice and restoring justice. Without their devotion to each other, Anis al-Jalis and Nur al-Din would not have fled from Basra to Baghdad, and Harun al-Rashid would not have found out about the conduct of al-Mu'in b. Sawi and removed him from office. 'Anis al-Jalis and Nur al-Din' resembles 'The Fisherman and the Demon' in another aspect. Harun al-Rashid relies on his good officers to maintain harmony in the community he rules. The king of Basra, al-Zaynabi, mirrors Harun al-Rashid. In the Harun al-Rashid myths, love takes on an additional meaning and function. It is at the heart of compassion and magnanimity.

Unlike Shahriyar, however, Harun al-Rashid and the king of Basra overlook or forgive certain trespasses. We have already witnessed the magnanimity of Harun al-Rashid. Al-Zaynabi also overlooks the Khaqan family's violation of his trust. Harun al-Rashid shows Shahriyar by example that love can guide anger into forgiveness and mercy, and, more importantly, educate passion into love and loyalty in love. That their power and grace are not unconditional speaks to the role of loyalty in love in communal harmony. Their authority is premised on the exclusive devotion of the lovers to each other. Nur al-Din's only virtue is his devotion to Anis al-Jalis.[9]

In the *Nights* stories, as we will see in more detail in Chapter 4, monogamy is coeval with loyalty and solidarity associated with brotherhood and friendship in the *Nights* and *adab*. Its ideology must underpin the imagined ideal community and serve as the code of conduct for all its members. Its opposite, the unrestrained pursuit of sex, with disregard for this code of conduct, inevitably leads to the disintegration of community. We have already seen in the Solomon legends in Chapter 1 and in the Harun al-Rashid myths in this chapter that this code of conduct matters more than the king, for in the *Nights* frame story, and in 'The Fisherman and the Demon', the king loses his kingdom when he or his queen violates this code.

Loyalty in Love, Family in Community

The centrality of loyalty in love between man and woman, or husband and wife, in the coherence of both family and community, which is implied in the Solomon legends and made more explicit in the Harun al-Rashid myths, gains focus in two overlapping genres of storytelling, also integrated into the *Nights*: 'romance' and 'epic'. The love stories in these two genres show that marital betrayal leads to the disintegration of community, as we have seen in the *Nights* frame story, the Solomon legends, and the Harun al-Rashid myths. However, they go further in linking the suitability of the union to political fortunes: a proper and appropriate union cements the legitimacy and continuity of a house of power, and the preservation and prosperity of a community.

These love stories are similarly informed by the ideology of monogamy inherent in the Solomon legends and the Harun al-Rashid myths, but these stories follow different narrative patterns. Two types of romance and epic love stories exist side by side and converse in the *Nights*. Whereas 'erotic romance' tends to follow the adventures of a pair of lovers from the time they fall in love and become separated until they finally reunite, 'patrimonial romance' stories detail the political fortunes of a kingly family and are centred more particularly on the cohesion of a kingdom.[10] These two types of love stories are intricately and inextricably inter-twined, the fate of the kingdom often being dependent on the resolution of the love story. The legitimacy of the kingdom is determined by the propriety of the union of the lovers which leads to triumph and the cohesion of empire, epic, and its impropriety results in the disinteg-ration of empire and wandering, romance.

''Umar al-Nuʿman and His Two Sons', a *sira* or mini-epic in the *Nights*,[11] exhibits the features of romance and epic.[12] The *sira* begins as a romance, or narrative of the defeated: a series of aimless wanderings of the 'heroes' whose poten-tials remain unrealised as the family, a metaphor for the nation, falls apart. However, what started out as a romance ends as an epic with the narrat-ive of the victors and the emergence of the 'hero', who unites his family and nation, and leads them to triumph, repossessing the lands taken by Christians. The turning point is located in a cycle of love stories inserted between the two parts of this *sira* whereby defeat turns into victory, and romance is transformed into epic. This epical turn is conditioned on the reunion and unity of the members of the kingly family, and the return to cohesion of the royal genealogy.

The first part of the *sira* recounts the beginning of the end of the kingdom of ʿUmar al-Nuʿman. It details the mortal sins committed by ʿUmar al-Nuʿman and his sons: lust, jealousy, greed, rape, incest, and treachery. The excesses of ʿUmar al-Nuʿman and his first-born, Sharrkan (or Shirkan), lead to the collapse of the kingdom. ʿUmar al-Nuʿman's two other children by a slave-girl, Daww al-Makan and Nuzhat al-Zaman, are doomed to leave home and wander. This section ends with ʿUmar al-Nuʿman and Sharrkan dying, and Daww al-Makan as a king under siege.

In the second part of the *sira*, Daww al-Makan dies, leaving the kingdom in the hands of outsiders. The narrative takes a drastic turn when it begins to tell the story of Kan-Ma-Kan, the son of Daww al-Makan. Orphaned, reduced to poverty, his kingdom usurped, and his union with his intended Qudiya-Fa-Kan prevented by a pretender king, Kan-Ma-Kan leaves to seek his fortune in the desert. On this journey, he is transformed from child to adult, victim to hero, and returns to Baghdad triumphantly. There he escapes an assassination attempt, amasses the support of all the Muslims with the help of the family's loyal vizier Dandan, and marries his cousin Qudiya-Fa-Kan. He further unites the Muslims and leads the newly assembled Muslim army towards Christian lands. More importantly, he finds his lost family and together they restore cohesion to the kingdom bequeathed by 'Umar al-Nu'man.

Between the two parts of the *sira*, two love stories are inserted. Dandan, the vizier, tells Daww al-Makan these stories at the peak of the latter's despair. Like all the *Nights* stories, these are stories within stories. At the outset, there is 'Taj al-Muluk and Dunya', and within this, ''Aziz and 'Aziza'. These are framed within the narrative of ''Umar al-Nu'man', which is in turn framed within the narrative of 'Shahrazad and Shahriyar'. The frame. 'Taj al-Kuluk', is the story of a king and his son and their quest for a suitable bride, and the framed, ''Aziz and 'Aziza', is the story of a pair of star-crossed lovers.

King Sulayman, king of 'The Green City', late in life marries a suitable bride, the daughter of the king of 'The White Land'. They have a son with kingly qualities, Taj al-Muluk, who is more enamoured with hunting than maidens. When King Sulayman exerts pressure on him to marry, to continue the family line, Taj al-Muluk runs away and goes on a hunting trip from which he does not intend to return. He meets a melancholic 'Aziz, who tells him about Dunya, with whom 'Aziz is in love but with whom he can no longer pursue a meaningful relationship. Taj al-Muluk falls instantly in love with Dunya.

He is intrigued by the condition of 'Aziz and persists with his questioning until 'Aziz tells him the story of his ill-fated love with his cousin and intended bride, 'Aziza, whom he actually

abandons on their wedding night. Instead, and
with the now miserable ʿAziza's help, he secures
the favours of Bint Dalila al-Muhtala and moves
in with her. ʿAziza then dies of a broken heart.
ʿAziz subsequently leaves Bint Dalila when he
falls in love with her nemesis. When Bint Dalila
finds him again, she castrates him and leaves
him for dead. Upon hearing the story of ʿAziz,
Taj al-Muluk embarks on a journey in pursuit of
Dunya's love.

'Taj al-Muluk' and "ʿAziz and ʿAziza' mirror
the two parts of "Umar al-Nuʿman' but in reverse
order. The story of "ʿAziz and ʿAziza' and the
first half of "Umar al-Nuʿman' are both structured round the trope of desire gone awry, while
the story of 'Taj al-Muluk' and the second half of
the epic is driven by the trope of educating
desire into love. Love, in the vocabulary of
pre-modern Arabic-Islamic theory of love, is the
right combination of reciprocal sexual desire,
commitment and loyalty (which is what binds
Taj al-Muluk and Dunya, and Kan-Ma-Kan and
Qudiya-Fa-Kan), not the pursuit of unbridled
passion alone (which is what ails ʿUmar
al-Nuʿman and ʿAziz). ʿAziz realises the true
meaning of love when he has lost everything
and remembers ʿAziza's words: 'Loyalty is beautiful, and treachery is ugly'.[13]

Love is Propriety in Conduct
As we have seen in Chapter 1, love can disable
the workings of reason, ʿaql, in its excessive
form, ʿishq, unbridled passion born of and

driven by sexual desire, and lead to madness, *junun*. Madness in this case means that passion veils reason and the lover no longer comprehends what is beneficial or harmful to him. What is at stake for the pre-modern theorist of love is the future of the Muslim in this life and hereafter; for love can be his ruination in this life when he becomes a danger to himself and his community, and his displacement from Heaven when he becomes mindless to the teachings of Islam. Love then must not remain unbridled passion; rather, it must be guided and developed by reason into something more. But what is reasonable love?

First, propriety must be observed. Love between man and woman must lead to social cohesion in the form of marriage. Marriage is a social responsibility and legal measure, and a good match, or proper love, must observe compatibility in looks and manners, as well as equivalence in social standing. Second, the taxonomy of love between man and woman is important too. The couple must behave in a fashion appropriate to lovers and generate reciprocal desire. Third, the union must take place lawfully. And fourth, most importantly, love must be vigilantly maintained through loyalty, patience, and endurance.[14]

The story of King Sulayman's marriage, with which 'Taj al-Muluk and Dunya' begins, serves as the basic model for a proper love match. The king patiently waits until a compatible princess (the daughter of an equal king) is found, and as is appropriate he falls in love with her on their wedding night when he comes face to face with her, his equal. 'Taj al-Muluk' follows this pattern but fleshes out the protocol of proper love. He is not patient like King Sulayman, and runs away when he is pressured to marry, but as soon as he falls in love, he pursues Dunya in a single-minded fashion.

Taj al-Muluk's is the story of prince-meets-princess and is deserving of a happy ending for having observed all the protocols of proper love. He conducts himself properly as a lover. When Dunya and her father refuse him, he pines for his beloved, loses his appetite for food, becomes an insomniac, and weeps whenever his beloved is remembered. He endures his heartache and patiently woos her until she falls in love with him too. He waits until it is both appropriate and legal for him to consummate his desire. More importantly, he generates desire in Dunya, who in turn behaves properly. When she falls in love with him, she does not give in to her desire immediately but waits for the right moment for their union, when they are legally married. She too displays loyalty towards her beloved and puts his wellbeing above her own. When her father raises his sword intent on killing Taj al-Muluk, she throws herself in front of it, crying 'kill me before you kill him!' Theirs is a story of desire that leads to love, and love that leads to desire.

The happy ending of their story should then be taken for granted, for what could go wrong in a story that observes all the proper requirements of reasonable love? The moral of their story is highlighted by its counter-story, ''Aziz and 'Aziza', the story of innocent devotion wasted on a self-indulgent young man who comes to a bad end, in which love is sabotaged by the mindless and improper desire of 'Aziz for Bint Dalila and her nemesis, and 'Aziza dies of unrequited love, unable to generate desire for her on 'Aziz's part.

Love is Kingly Genealogy

The moral of a love story might end here but that of an epic could not, for in an epic it is not the fate of the lovers that is at stake but rather that of a community, a fate determined by the vibrant continuity of royal genealogy and kingship. The successful union of lovers is only the first step towards the preservation of the community. The maintenance of kingship requires more than requited love, as shown by the love stories incorporated into the ''Umar al-Nu'man' story.

The possible love stories contained in the first half of the *sira* appear improper, illegitimate and incomplete. A potential love story between a seemingly well-matched couple, Sharrkan and Ibriza, the daughter of a rival Christian king, is never fully realised in the absence of desire. While we are still haunted by the promise of their love, Ibriza is suddenly paired with 'Umar al-Nu'man through rape. This is a case of passion gone awry and the rape – improper, illegal, and almost incest – generates life as well as death: Ibriza dies while giving birth to a son. There is, moreover, an incestuous love affair between Sharrkan and his half-sister Nuzhat al-Zaman. The liaison, despite the birth of a child, Qudiya-Fa-Kan, ends unhappily as soon as their blood relationship is revealed: Nuzhat al-Zaman is hastily married off to Sharrkan's chamberlain to conceal the incest from King ʿUmar al-Nuʿman.

In contrast, the love story in the second half of the *sira* develops differently. Kan-Ma-Kan, his throne usurped by the former chamberlain – the pretender father of Qudiya-Fa-Kan – is prevented from seeing his beloved. He pines as befitting a lover, then leaves to seek his fortune, transforms into a hero, and returns to reclaim his throne, defeat his enemies, reunite his family, and marry Qudiya-Fa-Kan. This love story, like that of Taj al-Muluk and Dunya, is proper, legitimate and perfect.

Where ''Aziz and ʿAziza' is situated in the *Nights* – within 'Taj al-Muluk', which is in turn inserted in ''Umar al-Nuʿman', which is further framed by the story of Shahriyar and Shahrazad – is thus instructive. The story of ʿAziz reminds Taj al-Muluk that he needs to find love to generate life. The story of ʿAziz, together with the counsel of Taj al-Muluk, shows Daww al-Makan that anguish (*jazaʿ*) alone will not turn defeat into triumph, and that in time – with persistence and patience – his kingdom will be restored. Taj al-Muluk indeed falls in love with Dunya, and through patience, and guided by ʿAziz, he is able to eventually marry her. Thus, Taj al-Muluk's kingdom is anticipated to continue.

These stories, together with the Solomon legends and the Harun al-Rashid myths, show Shahriyar that betrayal (*ghadr*), and the knee-jerk reaction to his anguish – both in terms of what has been inflicted upon him and what he has been meting out against his people – will lead to the annihilation of his entire community. The story of ʿAziza offers the meaning of true love, which is loyalty and patience. Through ʿAziza's love, during her life and after her death, ʿAziz comes to understand the meaning of love, and is enabled to know his true heart, ʿAziza, goes on living and, in fact, even falls in love.

Here, the storytellers of the three stories, ʿAziza, Dandan, and Shahrazad, merge into one. They set themselves as examples. While Shahrazad tells Shahriyar endless tales night after night at the peak of his anguish, the vizier Dandan tells Daww al-Makan the story of another kingly family when the latter is in despair over the survival of his kingdom, and ʿAziza tells ʿAziz love stories when he is desperately pining after Bint Dalila. These stories are the means by which the tides of misfortune are turned around. Taj al-Muluk finds his mate and starts a family. Daww al-Makan returns to Baghdad, his offspring, Kan-Ma-Kan, unites his kingdom and restores its cohesion, and Shahriyar pardons Shahrazad as well as his own community. More importantly, life is generated again.

Chapter 3

Harmonious Community: Fathers and Mothers, Sons and Daughters

And remember David and Solomon, when they gave judgement regarding the field.

(Q. 21: 78)

The Qur'anic verse refers to a famous story in which Solomon disagreed with his father about a judgement that David rendered. David yielded to Solomon's judgement in this instance, deferring to his son's wisdom and making way for the latter to take over the leadership of the community. That fathers, a shorthand for forefathers in the Qur'an, cede to the wisdom and authority of the son is integral to the message of Islam. Muhammad's prophecy, like those of earlier prophets, is a corrective to the erring ways of the fathers and forefathers, and as such it replaces existing traditions and practices.

Father figures come in two forms, either a man furious at losing his power who wreaks havoc for the son before he retreats into the background; or a benevolent patriarch too old and feeble to protect his son. Muhammad's uncles and the elderly of Mecca represent the former, and Jacob, Joseph's loving father, the latter. These two figures are abstracted into two archetypes in storytelling around the world: the absent and the tyrannical father. Such an abstraction fits well with the logic of epic and romance, for the hero in these two genres is usually cast as an orphan who rises to power and builds an ideal community through his own journey of maturation supported only by his beloved, as we have seen in the previous chapters, and a community of like-minded people, his close companions and friends, as we shall see in the next chapter.

Kan-Ma-Kan in "Umar al-Nu'man', and Frodo and Aragorn in *The Lord of the Rings* are examples of the first archetype. They are all orphans. Daww al-Makan, Kan-Ma-Kan's father, dies before he can restore his father's kingdom. Frodo is raised by his uncle, Bilbo, and Aragorn is fostered by

Figure 15. Frodo Baggins (Elijah Wood) and his uncle Bilbo (Ian Holm), in the film adaptation of *The Lord of the Rings: The Fellowship of the Ring* (Peter Jackson, 2001).

the elven, having lost his father at the age of two. Another magical hero and household name, Harry Potter, similarly loses his parents as an infant and is entrusted to his maternal aunt. Their orphanhood often signals not only the break-up of their biological family but also of the community they live in. Aragorn loses his parents to Sauron and his forces. Harry Potter's parents die to protect their newborn from Voldemort. Even more heroes of Arabic story-telling suffer from the absence of a father who might offer a firm guiding hand. The titular protagonists of 'Aladdin' and 'Hasib Karim al-Din' in the *Nights* also lose their fathers at a young age.

'Umar al-Nu'man represents the second archetype. He is the epitome of the tyrannical father in the Arabic tradition of epic and romance. 'Antara in *Sirat 'Antara* and al-Battal in *Sirat al-Amira Dhat al-Himma*, to name but two, have to both free themselves from their fathers' strategies of control and exploitation, and on occasion to fight against them. Incest in ''Umar al-Nu'man', as we saw in the preceding chapter, is a sure forecast of the disintegration of a community, for kings and queens are fathers and mothers of the community in Arabic and Chinese storytelling.

Sovereigns are Fathers and Mothers of the Community

A sovereign and a father are both responsible for justice and communal harmony at home and in society. In Chinese, the Confucian *wulun*, 'sovereign and courtier' and 'father and son' relationships overlap. The idea that the queen is the mother of the community is found in the Chinese expression *muyi tianxia* and in Arabic and Chinese stories about empresses, queens, and consorts. Khadija is regarded as the mother of the Muslim community. 'The consorts of the caliphs', such as Zubayda, are expected to look after every member of her community like her children. More recently, as we see in Mahmoud Darwish's famous poem, 'To My Mother', the Palestinian homeland is mapped onto the figure of his mother. The bread she bakes and coffee she brews for her family sustain not only her children but also the nation ('Dearly I yearn for my mother's bread, my mother's coffee').

Parent and child are expected to follow a code of conduct appropriate to an ideal community governed by love and reason, care and loyalty, and fairness in managing rights and wrongs. Fathers and mothers play a leading role in the drama of community making in which the parent and child relationship – be it 'father and son', 'father and daughter', 'mother and son', or 'mother and daughter' – plays a central role in the coherence or disintegration of a community.

Historical Chinese emperors and empresses have, like Harun al-Rashid, become myths in Chinese culture and literature in the telling and retelling of their stories. More importantly, they are iconized as fathers and mothers of the community, and as such their conduct towards

Figure 16. Scene from *The Adventures of Prince Achmed*, by Lotte Reiniger. The oldest surviving feature-length animated film, *Prince Achmed* was inspired by the *Nights*.

their children confirms their legitimacy, or lack thereof, as family and community leaders.

A famous example is Cao Cao (155–220 CE) whose legitimacy is challenged in the canonical classic Chinese novel *Three Kingdoms* by Luo Guanzhong (d. 1440). He is here portrayed as a father who divides and conquers his own sons, leading ultimately to the collapse of his kingdom – we shall return to this work in Chapter 4. His despotism is magnified in the 2008–2009 epic war film *Red Cliff* directed by John Woo, adapted from an episode in *Three Kingdoms*. The title of the film refers to a battle of the same name between the three kingdoms, Wei, Shu, and Wu, that were established in the shadow of the collapsing Han Dynasty (202 BCE to 220 CE). In this film, Cao is not only a womanizer, but also a ruthless statesman and father.

Illegitimate emperors in Chinese stories are portrayed as mirror images of Cao. The two emperors in the Chinese television dramas, *Nirvana in Fire* I (2015) and II (2017), are good examples. In I, the emperor–father is a despot obsessed with power. He kills his loyal generals and turns his sons against each other to consolidate his power. The legitimate reigns of his son and grandson are different. They foster close bonds and rule their empire lovingly. We see the solidarity between the grandson and his brother in II.

Empress Wu Zetian (r. 665–705), the only empress to rule the Tang Dynasty (618–907), is another example of a historical figure being iconized into a model ruler in Chinese storytelling. Neither her character nor her ascent to power was controversy free. Stories about a concubine of the first Tang emperor, Taizong (r. 626–649), who married the emperor's son, Gaozong (r. 649–683) and became an empress, never cease. These stories, such as the popular television series *Wu Zetian* (1995) and *Wu Meiniang* (2014), are full of clandestine affairs, rumours of cruelty, conspiracy theories and palace intrigues.

At the same time, they put Empress Wu on the pedestal of *muyi tianxia* (mother of the nation). In a popular trilogy of Detective Dee films (2010–2018), adapted from stories about Empress Wu's chancellor, Di Renjie (d. 704), we see Dee's ambivalence towards Empress Wu transform into respect and loyalty as he is won over by her fair, intelligent, and tough rule. Empress Wu comes across as a strong and benevolent mother, even in the physical presentation of her character.

We see a parallel iconization of Harun al-Rashid and Zubayda in two stories anthologized in the tenth-century *Tales of the Marvellous and News of the Strange*: 'Muhammad the Foundling and Harun al-Rashid' and 'The Story of Ashraf and Anjab and the Marvellous Things That Happened to Them'. These stories demonstrate the ways in which a parent's role overlaps with that of a sovereign. The sovereign here refers to both Harun al-Rashid and his queen consort, Zubayda. Motherhood and fatherhood need not be biological, and the latter is about a father's duty of care towards his family and community.

Muhammad the Foundling

During one of his nocturnal journeys in Baghdad, accompanied by his vizier Jaʿfar and his eunuch Masrur, Harun al-Rashid went to one of his many gardens to enjoy a night of music. Masrur hears a cry, goes to investigate, and finds a beautiful baby:

> By its head was a purse containing a thousand dinars, and a note had been left on its breast. The baby itself was more radiant

than the rising sun, and on its forehead was a circle of pearls, each five carats in weight, gleaming like stars.

He brings the baby back to Harun al-Rashid together with the note that read:

> Whoever finds this child should treat him with respect for the sake of Almighty God, as he comes from the greatest of families. His mother died, and this world is the home of misery. The thousand dinars are for his upbringing, and whoever rears him can expect Paradise as a reward from the Greatest and Glorious God. He has been put to shelter into this splendid garden.[1]

Upon reading the note, Harun al-Rashid weeps and tells his vizier Jaʿfar to take the baby to Zubayda, who names him Muhammad the Foundling and raises him, treating him like her own flesh and blood. In fact, Muhammad the Foundling is sure he is one of al-Rashid's own children – he is always playing with al-Amin and al-Muʿtasim, and getting himself into trouble, only for Harun al-Rashid to come to his rescue.

'The Story of Muhammad the Foundling' is a reminder not only of parents' duty of care towards their children, but also of a sovereign's responsibility towards his subjects. The three episodes comprising the story tackle the shared responsibility of parent and sovereign. As a father, he has a duty of care towards his son. In the first episode, he forgets all about Muhammad, until he is reminded. The reminder is loud. While playing polo with al-Amin and al-Muʿtasim, Muhammad hits the ball so hard that it flies up from the pitch and rebounds from the roof of the hall of the new palace of Harun al-Rashid and strikes the dome before falling back to the ground. An alarmed Harun al-Rashid sends the eunuch Masrur to investigate. Harun al-Rashid then discovers that this adopted son has grown up into a beautiful boy under Zubayda's care and has mastered music and the lute. He decides to keep this 'son of choice', who 'is better than a real one', for good.

The second episode involves a jealous slave-girl who, like Zulaykha in the Qur'anic story of Joseph, tries to seduce Muhammad the Foundling and when she fails, accuses him of rape. Harun al-Rashid is angry – this Christian slave-girl was given to him as a gift – and while in a drunken stupor he orders Masrur to kill Muhammad without any investigation. When he wakes, he regrets his orders. He has disappointed his son as a father, and his subject as a sovereign. He finds out that the slave-girl had lied, but it is too late. However, Masrur has not killed Muhammad but left him in the desert to fend for himself; he is rescued and travels to Basra, where he is taken in by Khultukh, the attendant of the governor, Muhammad al-Zaynabi, who is a cousin of Harun al-Rashid.

The third and final episode redeems Harun al-Rashid but with a twist. When Masrur finally

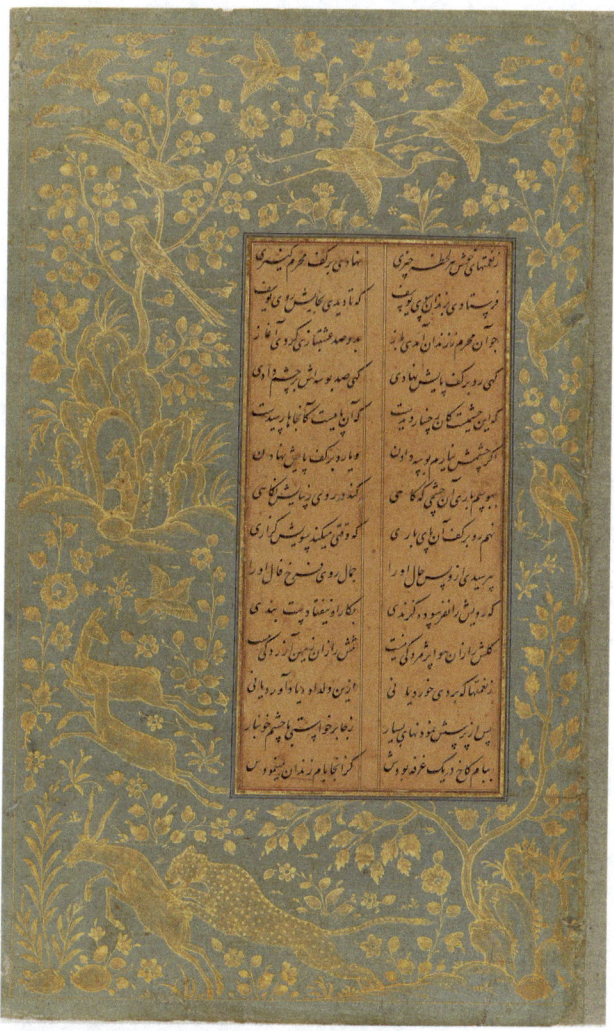

Figure 17. Folio from a manuscript of *Yusuf and Zulaykha*.

finds Muhammad the Foundling in Basra and brings him home to Harun al-Rashid, Muhammad now recognizes Khultukh as his adoptive father. After all, Khultukh had looked after him and even put his properties and belongings under Muhammad's disposal. Khultukh leaves his house in a rush when he hears rumours that the governor he serves, Muhammad al-Zaynabi, is about to arrest him. He goes to Baghdad to look for Muhammad the Foundling. He is reunited with his adopted son, and has an audience with Harun al-Rashid. Harun al-Rashid summons Muhammad al-Zaynabi to Baghdad and resolves the misunderstanding. Kultukh decides to sell his house in Basra and remain in Baghdad to be close to Muhammad the Foundling. Harun al-Rashid happily keeps both as his close companions, rewarding them for being good. 'This is the reward for good deeds,' the story ends with this and two lines of poetry:

Who acts well never goes without reward;
And kindness is not lost with God or man.[2]

Harun al-Rashid may be a good caliph here, a ruler who rights wrongs, but he pales by comparison as a father. His comparators are Khultukh and, of course, his wife Zubayda. Motherhood, like fatherhood, is not dictated by blood but by care. Zubayda looks after Muhammad the Foundling without fail and treats him like Harun al-Rashid's other children. She is instrumental in Muhammad the Foundling's education, ensuring that he should be educated to be an upright person and, more importantly, with a skill that would please Harun al-Rashid. It is almost as if she is the mother of the community, and Harun al-Rashid the father. Their duty of care, as father and mother of the community, as will be seen in 'The Story of Ashraf and Anjab', encompasses the entire community.

Al-Ashraf and al-Anjab

On one of his visits to Baghdad, Muhammad al-Zaynabi falls in love with a slave-girl, 'Alam al-Husn, whom he had purchased for Harun al-Rashid for three thousand dinars. When he takes her to Zubayda, she learns of his feelings and tells him to take her with him to Basra and marry her. He does and a son, al-Ashraf, is born to them. A black slave-girl, the mother of a one-year-old boy, al-Anjab, is employed to nurse al-Ashraf. Al-Anjab grows up believing he is al-Ashraf's brother. Muhammad al-Zaynabi indeed treats both like his sons, having 'taught [both of them] to write, literature, grammar, Arabic and everything they might need' as well as 'how to ride, shoot, and act courageously'. Muhammad al-Zaynabi dies, but he leaves a note written in his own hand that states:

> I am Muhammad son of Sulayman al-Zaynabi. The only child of my body is my son al-Ashraf, the inheritor of my wealth and the perpetuator of my race. As for the black al-Anjab, I bought him and his mother for

eighteen dinars. He is my son's slave, to be
sold or freed as my son wishes, and no one is
to suspect me of being his father.[3]

Al-Anjab is greedy and wants to inherit
Muhammad al-Zaynabi's position. Al-Ashraf,
on the other hand, is generous and magnanimous. He refuses to sell al-Anjab and his mother.
Instead, he divides his father's possessions
equally between them. Al-Anjab kills his mother
to keep his identity secret, goes to Baghdad, and
succeeds in plotting against the vizier, present-
ing himself as Muhammad al-Zaynabi's son.
Although Zubayda is incredulous – Muhammad
al-Zaynabi was white and the slave-girl he had
married was also white, nonetheless, Harun
al-Rashid appoints al-Anjab as his vizier. In the
meantime, al-Ashraf spends all his money on
friends and the poor and comes to Baghdad to
seek his brother's help. Al-Anjab puts him in a
dungeon instead.

Al-Ashraf's surrogate father, 'Ubayd, comes
to his rescue. 'Ubayd had been looking after
al-Ashraf since his arrival in Baghdad. He now
entrusts to his elderly mother the task of bringing food to the imprisoned al-Ashraf and travels
to Basra to seek 'Alam al-Husn. He finds her and
brings her to Baghdad. He returns to his craft as
a cook, and she begins to work as a washer-
woman. In time she befriends one of Harun
al-Rashid's eunuchs, Yanis, who admires her
beauty and skills as a washer-woman and, more
importantly, as a lute player.

'Alam al-Husn ends up in Harun al-Rashid's palace at one of his parties, and purposefully breaks one of his precious cups. She is brought before Harun al-Rashid. She tells him who al-Ashraf is and how his slave as well as brother, al-Anjab, betrayed him. Harun al-Rashid of course rewards al-Ashraf and punishes al-Anjab. Al-Ashraf is appointed vizier in al-Anjab's stead, and al-Anjab is beheaded. Harun al-Rashid of course behaves like a sovereign, punishing evil and righting wrong. His decisiveness in executing al-Anjab may be contrasted with al-Ashraf's refusal to exact this type of revenge on someone he thinks of as his brother. Brotherhood is not just a matter of blood, as we will see in the next chapter. He and al-Anjab drank from the same woman's milk, and in Arabic-Islamic culture, a mother's milk is as thick as blood.

Role of Mothers: Jullanar

Mothers play an additional role as the caretakers of sons and daughters especially in the absence of fathers. There are no tyrannical mothers in Arabic storytelling. Their role is, however, similarly paradoxical. They are either caring but hapless, like Aladdin's and Hasib Karim al-Din's mothers, or role models who are at the same time firm guiding hands, such as Jullanar.

'Jullanar of the Sea', found in both the *Nights* and the *Tales of the Marvellous and News of the Strange*, is the story of a mother educating her son by example and action. It does so by overlapping two stories, that of Princess Jullanar and her husband, King Shahriman, and that of their son, King Badr, and his beloved, Princess Jawhara. The story begins with childless King Shahriman giving up all his concubines and marrying Jullanar. A beautiful son is soon born. Shahriman later dies, leaving his fifteen-year-old son to rule over his kingdom. The rest of the story sees the fatherless Badr, like all epic heroes, go through a trying journey of learning how to be king. In pursuit of desire for its own sake, he becomes lost in passion and wanders around the world. As soon as he reins in his desire and learns to love properly, he returns home and becomes king.

'The Story of Jullanar' is made up of two distinct parts, each of a different genre notwithstanding the genealogical continuity. The short first part is a love story about the eponymous sea princess who, after a quarrel with her brother, Salih, runs away from home determined to marry the first worthy landman she meets. She is sold to Shahriman, an elderly and good king who is pining for an heir. It is love at first sight for the king. A year and nine months later, she gives birth to a son, Badr.

The twice-as-long second part is a love quest or, more appropriately, an adventure. Shahriman is now dead, and Badr is king. He must marry, Salih advises his sister Jullanar, and a suitable bride must be found. But who is worthy of her son, the queen frets, the best of both worlds, the sea and the land? Salih suggests a sea princess, Jawhara. Badr falls in love with his uncle's description of Jawhara. He leaves without his mother's knowledge, abandoning his duty as king, and follows his uncle to the sea. From that moment passion reigns supreme and things spiral out of control.

They go to Jawhara's father, King al-Samandal, who laughs scornfully at their proposal and threatens Salih. Salih unleashes his army on al-Samandal and in the end captures and imprisons him. Alas, Jawhara has fled from the mayhem, and Badr haplessly follows suit and catches up with her. She, of course, will never marry the cause of her homelessness and, more to the point, without proper protocol. She transforms him into a bird and leaves him to his fate. He returns to human form only to be ship-wrecked, captured, and bewitched by Queen Lab. He escapes being transformed into a mule only to be recaptured, turned into a hideously ugly bird, and imprisoned in a cage. Finally, a sympathetic slave-girl sneaks him back to his mother, Jullanar. Suddenly, all is well again. Jullanar restores Badr to his human form and defeats his captor. Finally, King al-Samandal and Jawhara agree to the marriage proposal.

The stark contrast between the two parts of the story is telling. The sedate and serene marriage of Shahriman and Jullanar on land is the epitome of reason – Shahriman is known as *'aqil*. The tumultuous courtship of Badr and Jawhara is, on the other hand, *ahmaq*, just like al-Samandal. The tumult ends only when Jullanar, the mother, retrieves her son and returns with him to Shahriman's kingdom, now his. While love and reason underpin the first part of 'Jullanar', desire and passion drive the narrative of the second half. *'Aql*, the law of ideal community, is manifest in Shahriman and Jullanar's love, and *hamaqa*, the rule of its opposite, al-Farabi's ignorant or sinful city, is *hawa* exemplified by all the characters living their passions to the hilt. In their passionate life, they are in danger of losing *'aql* altogether.

When Salih seeks Jawhara's hand for Badr, al-Samandal mocks him, 'Are you without reason to such a degree'; Salih in turn thinks of al-Samandal as *ahmaq* and finds him *ghafil* (unaware of the goings-on around him) when he returns with his army to take over the kingdom. Badr, on the other hand, loses his ability to artic-ulate and communicate, a feature of a human endowed with *'aql*, when he is repeatedly trans-formed into a bird, in fact, a bird with an unstoppable appetite for food. Here, *hamaqa*, associated with desire, anarchy, and war, is juxtaposed to *'aql*, the foundation of love, harmony, and peace.[4]

We find the same interplay between desire and love, passion and reason, betrayal and loyalty, and chaos and harmony in both *The Lord of the Rings* and *Harry Potter*. The dark worlds of Sauron and Voldemort, driven by unchecked desire for power, wreak havoc in the harmony of Frodo and Harry Potter's communities, while Aragorn and Harry Potter, as well as their friends and allies, grow and mature into the community leaders. They learn along the way, to realise, as Harry Potter shouts at Voldemort in their first showdown, "You are the weak one. You'll never know love or friendship."[5]

It is the love of his friends that helps Frodo to let go of the ring, Aragorn to pick up his father's sword and take on the responsibility of kingship, and Harry Potter to defeat Voldemort. In the final battle between Harry Potter and Voldemort, Harry Potter is poignantly supported by the presence of ghosts or memories of his parents and their best friends. Frodo and Harry Potter lead fellowships of men and women who follow the path of love, reason, and loyalty to defeat Sauron and Voldemort who pursue absolute power without regard for the good of the living beings and the world, and to restore peace and harmony in their communities.

The two parts of 'The Story of Jullanar' together show one important difference between love and desire. Father and son, Shahriman and Badr, have similar trajectories in their transformations into a befitting king. Shahriman, a 'sensible, discerning, and pious man who judged fairly between the strong and the weak and treated the offenders with mercy',[6] has only one weakness, his appetite for sex with his many women and concubines. He is without an heir until he learns to abandon the joy of sex for the commitment of responsible love. When he falls in love with Jullanar and becomes exclusively devoted to her, he is finally blessed with a son, Badr.

Badr begins as a good ruler, 'judging fairly between the strong and the weak and exacting from the prince the right of the beggar' but, like his father, he must first go mad with desire then learn love in order to become a true king.[7] The misadventures he experiences, albeit haplessly, educate him into being his father's true heir; he finally knows love, or is happily married. That desire is susceptible to love's education marks the story's distinction from 'the Enchanted King' and explains the two young kings' different destinies.

Jullanar is a paragon of reason and wisdom. As a wife, she tests Shahriman for a year before confessing that she returns his love and is with child; as a mother, she does not panic when her son goes missing but instead, patient and steadfast, returns to watch over his kingdom on his behalf. When at last she learns of her son's whereabouts she rescues him and restores him to the throne. More importantly, her relationship with her husband and her relationship with her son exemplify the ideal husband-and-wife as well as mother-and-son relationships.

At the heart of the story is, once again, educating desire into love, self-interest into loyalty to another, be that king, wife, brother, subject or community, that is fundamental to the legitimacy and effectiveness of kingship in the *Nights*. Fatherhood and motherhood are defined by devotion, care, and constancy.

Returning to the 'The Story of Ashraf and Anjab', ʿUbayd and ʿAlam al-Husn are a perfect match for each other. 'Ubayd is not al-Ashraf's biological father, but he is equal to his biological mother, 'Alam al-Husn, in dedication to and care for al-Ashraf. It makes sense, then, that in the end 'Ubayd asks only for 'Alam al-Husn's hand, turning down everything else Harun al-Rashid offers him. He prefers to return to his simple life as a cook and live happily ever after with his beloved rather than take up a position at court and reside in a palace.

Harun al-Rashid and Zubayda are a perfect couple as well but in a different sense. As father and mother of the community, their duty and care go beyond their immediate family and the harem embracing the entire community. Just like Harun al-Rashid, who in the Arabic stories about him is always ready to give up a slave-girl to reward the worthy, Zubayda willingly gives her slave-girls in marriage to a young man deserving of her love. They are the patriarch and matriarch of the community they rule, and the entire community is their family.

Such surrogate father and mother figures are abundant in storytelling worldwide. These replace biological parents in *The Lord of the Rings* and *Harry Potter*. Frodo finds a kind and generous father in Bilbo and a teacher and guide in Gandalf, the wizard. Aragon similarly finds alternative fathers in Gandalf and the elf Elrond. Harry Potter makes his alternative family with the Weasleys. While he looks up to Mr and Mrs Weasley as his parents, in fact he marries into the family, and they look after him like their own child. Of course, Professor Dumbledore is always there for him. The 'parent-child' and 'sibling' relationships that Frodo, Aragorn and Harry Potter forge with Bilbo and Gandalf, Elrond and Gandalf, the Weasleys and Dumbledore, provide them with an alternative ideal community, which now overlaps with 'friendship', the basis for an alternative society in which biological families can return and prosper again.

Chapter 4

Alternative Society: The Fellowship of Men and Women

> Not only Robin himself but all the band were outlaws and dwelled apart from other men, yet they were beloved by the country people round about, for no one ever came to jolly Robin for help in time of need and went away again with an empty fist.
>
> Howard Pyle, *The Merry Adventures of Robin Hood* (1883)

We have already caught a glimpse of the importance of friendship as a communal glue in *The Lord of the Rings* and *Harry Potter*. When the biological family is absent or dysfunctional, Frodo, Aragorn and Harry Potter find in their friends an alternative family, and when their familiar community gives in to the powers of darkness, Sauron and Voldemort, and its harmony disintegrates into conflict and war, they play a central role in uniting the forces of good and leading the effort to defeat evil and restore peace in the world.

The fellowship of the ring, a band of warriors who reject Sauron's ambitions to rule the world, accompany and protect Frodo on his journey to destroy the ring. This fellowship is complemented by a circle of Frodo's close hobbit friends: Samwise, Pippin, and Merry. Both groups are indispensable to Frodo's success. The fellowship and friendship of the two groups are marked by their quest for communal peace and harmony, alliance with forces of good, and loyalty to, and care for, each other. Harry Potter relies on his two closest friends, Ron Weasley and Hermione Granger, without whose support and help his triumph over Voldemort would not have been possible. Here, friendship overlaps with brotherhood and sisterhood. The Weasley siblings all play a key role in Harry Potter's journey to rid the world of Voldemort and restore harmony to it.

Brotherhood and sisterhood are also an important communal glue. When the brotherly or sisterly bond is broken in Arabic storytelling, tumult follows, particularly in the *Nights*, and an alternative must be found, or a reunion must be brought about before harmony can return. When the titular female protagonists of 'The Porter and Three Ladies of Baghdad' find themselves betrayed by their own flesh-and-blood sisters, their world and life fall apart. They turn to friends for support, replacing sisterhood with friendship as their alternative society. In 'al-Ashraf and al-Anjab', as we have seen in the previous chapter, when the bond of brotherhood is broken, the family disintegrates, and the suffering member of the family regains his equilibrium only when an alternative family is found or, as we read in another *Nights*' story, 'The Two Viziers', when a reunion takes place.

The Two Viziers

The story of 'The Two Viziers' begins in total harmony:

> ... a long time ago there lived in the province of Egypt a just, trusted, kind, generous, courageous, and powerful king, who associated with the learned and loved the poor. He had a wise, experienced, and influential vizier, who was careful, cautious, and skilled in the affairs of the state. This vizier, who was a very old man, had two sons who were like two moons or two lovely deer in their perfect elegance, beauty, and grace. [...] One day as it had been foreordained, their father the vizier died, and the king mourned him and summoned the two sons, bestowed on them robes of honor and other favors and said, "You shall take your father's place and be joint viziers of Egypt." [...] Then they assumed their position, taking turns, each performing his duty for a week at a time, and each accompanying the king on one journey at a time. The two lived in the same house and their world was one.[1]

Before lông, the two brothers fall out, not over affairs of state or their relationship, but over an imaginary scenario. The two brothers are happily chatting about their future, dreaming of marrying two sisters on the same day, and giving birth to sons and daughters. They will cement their family ties further by marrying their children to each other. But they quarrel over the issue of dowry, and in anger Nur al-Din, the younger brother, leaves and exiles himself all the way to Basra. There he establishes himself as the vizier of the King of Basra.

Shams al-Din, the older brother, marries and has a daughter, Sitt al-Husn; Nur al-Din does the same and has a son, Badr al-Din. Nur al-Din dies in Basra. Badr al-Din incurs his king's anger, his properties are confiscated and an order for his head is issued. Badr al-Din escapes and while in exile a naughty genie brings him to the wedding of his cousin, Sitt al-Husn. For having refused to marry the king, Sitt al-Husn is being forced to marry a hunchback. Badr al-Din weds his cousin in place of the hunchback, but the genie takes him away before dawn. A son, 'Ajib, is born. Badr al-Din wanders and ends up in Damascus as a cook. When 'Ajib encounters bullying, his grandfather, having heard the tale of Sitt al-Husn, decides to travel to Basra to look for his brother and nephew. They find Badr al-Din in Damascus and the family is reunited: 'the vizier and his nephew and daughter lived the best of lives in prosperity and ease, eating and drinking and enjoying themselves to the end of their days'.[2]

Friendship in Arabic-Islamic Writings

Not all families are as fortunate. The brothers in 'al-Ashraf and al-Anjab' and the sisters in 'The Porter and the Three Ladies of Baghdad' do not recover their blood relations. Brotherhood and sisterhood are replaced by friendship, which works as the communal glue in these two stories as well as others. There exists a long tradition of writing on friendship and companionship in Arabic, beginning with the Prophetic Tradition, through the conduct of his Companions in biographical literature and ending with the diverse and divergent theoretical treatises written by Muslim scholars in religious works or *adab*, or translated or adapted from Indian, Persian, or Greek sources. In this tradition of writing, even in the modern period, friendship and brotherhood are always linked.

Abu Hayyan al-Tawhidi (d. 1023), for example, points to the importance of friendship as underpinning the ideal human relationship, which itself serves as one of the foundations of ideal community in al-Farabi's 'Virtuous City'. The presence of friendship, as al-Tawhidi describes in his epistle on *al-Sadaqa wa'l-sadiq* (Friendship and Friends), indicates 'harmonious communal living' resulting from 'care of [each other], mutual protection, loyalty, help, advice, magnanimity, and consolation'.[3] These are exemplary human characteristics and are all signs of reason, *'aql*, and knowledge, *'ilm*,[4] or faith, *iman*. The absence of friendship points to the decline of loyalty and the corruption of human hearts, which are in turn signs of shortcoming and ignorance (or passion). Al-Tawhidi sees friendship as a cornerstone of political authority that defines and governs the relationship between the sovereign and his officers, among the government officers themselves, and between the government and its subjects (the people).[5]

Al-Tawhidi connects friendship with brotherhood in his epistle aimed at reforming man, community and political authority in such a way that both this life and the afterlife may be safeguarded, but like Arabic-Islamic writings in general he does not elaborate on the link between brotherhood and friendship or demonstrate how they overlap and underpin Arabic imaginings of an ideal community. However, the extensive Chinese writings on the subject can offer a blueprint for understanding the role of brotherhood and friendship in Arabic stories.

Friendship in Chinese Literature

Friendship is explicitly linked to brotherhood in Chinese poetry and story. Friendship plays a key role in the various imaginings of the ideal community. More importantly, Chinese writings articulate the overlap between brotherhood and friendship in their imaginings of ideal community. In Chinese writings, friendship has a pervasive presence in storytelling. Whereas during the Western Zhou Dynasty (11th century BCE to 771 BCE) the idea of family was in some ways similar to that of the Arab tribe, this changed during the Spring and Autumn Period (770–476 BCE), when the family began to be defined as more like today's 'nuclear' family and the contours of *wulun* relationships came to be clearly delineated.[6]

There were two opposing views with regard to friendship and family (inclusive of brotherhood) during the Warring States Period (475–221 BCE). While the Confucian philosopher Mencius (371–289 BCE) saw friendship as the ideal framework for the relationship between the ruler and his officers, the philosopher and statesman of the legalist school, Han Fei (280–233 BCE), saw the selfishness inherent in friendship as posing a danger to the relationship between the ruler and his officers, which must be underpinned by altruism, service, and the greater good. This view of friendship developed in parallel with the growth of family as central in the Confucian vision, whereby state and society are to be organized just like family, according to a hierarchy. The emperor, like the father, sits at the top of this hierarchy.

This dichotomy between friendship and family persisted until Ming China (1368–1644), when friendship became the fertile ground from which criticism of family was launched. The political and social structure based on family in Confucian thought demands the full obedience of individuals in all areas of life. The rules, manifest in customs and habits, can stifle individual voices, and on occasion even turn a blind eye to injustice.

Friendship and Brotherhood in Arabic and Chinese Storytelling

Friendship, as an alternative to family, opens up the political and moral landscape to individual freedom and rebellion against unjust rule. We can see the intersecting and conflicting

Figure 18. A stamp printed in China shows *The Outlaws of the Marsh*, circa 1991.

discourses on authority, familial, or dynastic, in Chinese storytelling which occupies a higher position in Chinese literature than its counterpart in Arabic storytelling. Two Chinese classic historical novels from the late Yuan Dynasty (1271–1368), *Three Kingdoms* and *Water Margin* (also known as *Outlaws of the Marsh*) are literary models or precursors of contemporary Chinese *wuxia* novels and *kung fu* films. Both explore friendship as an alternative framework for family and community, which tell us a great deal about the imagining of the ideal community in the subsequent Ming period.

Three Kingdoms
Friendship is one of the most important axes around which historical events are structured in

Three Kingdoms. It is overlapped with, as well as opposed to, family, which served as the core framework for state and political authority in China until the 1911 revolution. Political authority is passed on within a family, to a son, brother, grandson or other qualified member of the family. The legitimacy of political authority in this form of rule is derived from family not the other way around. Whoever possesses political authority has legitimacy as well. The crux of the matter in *Three Kingdoms*, one may argue, is to take control of the ruling family and through this to gain legitimacy of rule. This novel tells

Figure 19. Liu Bei, Guan Yu and Zhang Fei swore as brothers in a peach orchard, from *The Three Kingdoms*, attrib. Luo Guanzhong (1330–1400).

the stories of Cao Cao (155–220), Liu Bei (161–223) and Sun Quan (182–252), who take part in the race for political authority as the Han Dynasty (202 BCE–220 CE) comes to its end, until each establishes his own, albeit short-lived, kingdom. These both soon disintegrate and the Jin Dynasty (256–460 CE) would establish itself in their wake.

The novel comprises two discourses. At one level it seems to confirm that the Han (Liu) family is at the heart of political authority and its legitimacy. Whoever wishes to rule must derive his legitimacy from close association with the Han Dynasty; although each of them has the military and financial means to establish an independent kingdom on the lands under their control, neither has the legitimacy to do so. Cao seizes control of the heir to the throne, rules in his name, and expands his territories. In the meantime, Liu, a distant uncle of the ruling family, finds another heir and claims for him and himself the legitimacy of rule. As for Sun, he rules his own lands without making any claims and continues to pay homage to the Han Dynasty.

At another level, a second discourse, complementing and at the same time opposing the first discourse, revolves around friendship as brotherhood, exploring the efficacy of each as the corner stone of political authority. Friendship and brotherhood are, one may argue, a way of imagining an ideal relationship among men, or its opposite, by which kingdoms will either rise or fall.

The novel begins with Liu meeting Guan Yu (160–220) and Zhang Fei (d. 221) and ends with the demise of their Shu kingdom as they die one after the other. The friendship that develops among the three men, Liu, Guan, and Zhang, plays an important role in the vision of political authority. Friendship in this story is juxtaposed to brotherhood in the story of the Wei kingdom revolving around the Cao family. The brothers, sons of Cao, kill each other as they fight over the throne; their kingdom also falls at the end of the novel. The behaviour of the Cao brothers cannot be the foundation for kingship and political authority. Friendship and brotherhood are the two opposite poles in this double discourse on political authority and its legitimacy. Ideal friendship must match exemplary brotherhood that does not resemble the relationship of the Cao brothers.

At the outset of the novel, Liu, Guan, and Zhang arrive separately in Liu's hometown, and having developed a great love for each other, decide to become blood brothers and join the warlords who are purportedly fighting to restore just rule and proper political authority. They perform the ritual that elevates friendship to brotherhood, vowing to 'die on the same day', and promising to provide for each other the duties al-Tawhidi speaks of as 'care, preservation, loyalty, advice, help, generosity and consolation',[7] which they indeed exemplify in their conduct towards each other. The trajectory of friendship follows the path of ideal male-female love, beginning with a chance meeting, love at first sight, and loyalty. Ideal brotherhood in Chinese literary imaginary is above blood relations, brotherhood and family. At the same time, it demands of brotherhood by blood that it be the model for ideal friendship.

Water Margin

This dialectical or dialogical relationship between friendship and brotherhood repeats itself in *Water Margin*, set during the reign of Emperor Song Huizong (r. 1100–1126), but takes a more complex form. Staging a confrontation between 'friendship that swings between greed and fear' and 'ideal friendship-brotherhood', *Water Margin* examines the legitimacy of political authority based on the conduct of the officers of the Song court. The novel consists of the stories of 108 'heroes' (*haohan* in Chinese, good, or manly, men). Chief among them are 36 outlaws, including three women. They have either killed a family member who committed an act of betrayal that led to the demise of another family member or the entire family or were accused falsely of a crime by a corrupt officer of the court. These 108 *haohan* all, by chance or by design, end up in Liangsha, a mountain in Shandong. Once there, they decide to become brothers and perform the blood-brother ritual. They vow to serve the state by restoring justice in its realms.

The Liangshan *haohan* brothers bear some resemblance to Liu, Guan, and Zhang in *Three*

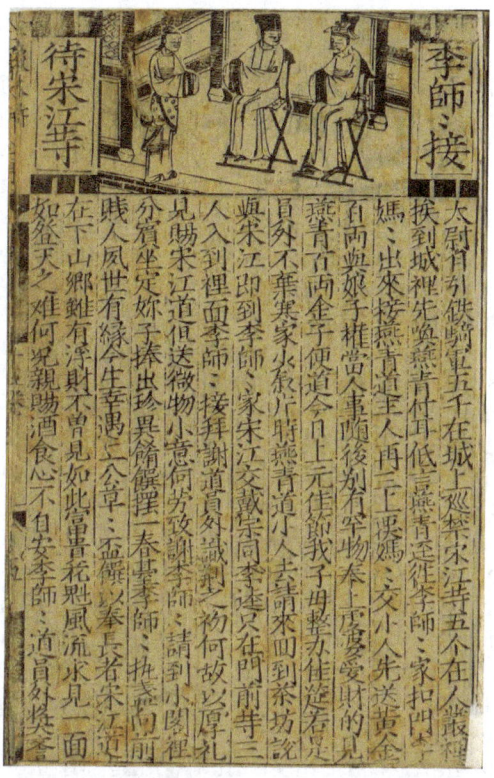

Figure 20. Shuihu Zhuan (*Water Margin*), Part 15 to 19, chapters 73 to 98 (hui). Block-print, dating from ca. 1600, brought to Denmark in the early part of the 17th c.

Kingdoms but also like Robin Hood and his merry men in Sherwood Forest. In these stories, it is entirely permissible for them to take the law into their own hands. The state's failure to uphold justice renders its legitimacy suspect and its laws subject to challenge. This additionally puts under scrutiny the concept of friendship–brotherhood proposed in *Three Kingdoms*. What shape does friendship take outside political authority? What about loyalty? Does it increase and decrease, and among whom? Does it have many faces? Do these faces conflict with each other? Can it alone serve as the foundation of a community? These are some of the questions *Water Margin* raises. And as we shall see, Arabic stories about *haohan*-like characters ask similar questions.

Water Margin is an amalgamation of stories collected from a variety of sources, including official history, popular history and storytelling and it went through several hands until the literati gave it, just like *Three Kingdoms*, its present shape. However, the novel takes an interest in minor historical characters and uses a language closer to the vernacular register. It also moves away from the centre of power, at court in the palace, and focuses on the margins of empire at a time of relative peace.

The heroes are more like young, strong men (*futuwwa*), larrikins (*shuttar*), and vagabonds (*'ayyarun*) in Islamic history, Arabic popular epics, and the *Nights*. Their skill in martial arts allows them to defeat the police or the army and run away should the need arise. They also have a reputation that precedes them, which facilitates their evasion of the authorities. They all have the following qualities: speed of action, generosity, ability to endure difficulties and hardship, abstinence from women, abhorrence of injustice and the unjust, readiness to help the downtrodden, decisiveness in taking matters into their own hands, willingness to become outlaws, and abiding by the principle of 'no obedience to the state in its disobedience of friendship'. Friendship, in these stories, is a symbol of justice.

Arabic Epics and the Thousand and One Nights

Six main figures in the *Nights* and popular Arabic epics have a great deal of affinity with the Chinese *haohan*: three men and three women respectively, Ahmad al-Danif, Hasan Shuman and 'Ali al-Zaybaq ('Ali the Mercury); and Dalila al-Muhtala (Dalila the Wily), her daughter Zaynab al-Nassaba (Zaynab the Deceitful), and 'Ali al-Zaybaq's mother, Fatima al-Fayyumiyya (from Fayyum in Egypt). Some are also mentioned in historical sources as real people. In the stories, however, these characters, usually described as *muhtal* (trickster), *shatir* (larrikin) or *'ayyar* (vagabond), are masters of disguise and of martial arts.

Their stories are, on the surface, about the tricks (played on others) to exact a payment of some sort. Upon closer scrutiny, they are shadowy figures, just like the Chinese *haohan*, who straddle two worlds, and only emerge from the underworld when the world is saturated with corruption. Their stories tell of the collusion and collision between the world and the underworld as part of an interrogation of justice. Does and can the law really dispense justice?

What is the limit of justice as defined by the law? Who are qualified to be officers of the law?

Each of the six characters mentioned above, all historical figures, may be the main protagonist in a story of their own but some also appear as a secondary character in stories of the others. These characters travel across the boundaries of history, the *Nights* and popular epics. The stories of these six figures overlap in the popular *al-sira al-sha'biyya* and the 19th-century versions of the *Nights*. Dalila al-Muhtala has a story devoted entirely to her exploits in the *Nights* and makes a major appearance in two other stories. We have already seen her as Bint Dalila al-Muhtala in ''Aziz and 'Aziza', one of the inset stories of the mini-epic of 'Umar al-Nu'man. She also plays the role of the nemesis of 'Ali al-Zaybaq. While Ahmad al-Danif and Hasan Shuman are the heroes in *Sirat Ahmad al-Danif*, they also appear as secondary characters in several other stories of the *Nights*.

These stories are all set in Baghdad during the reign of Harun al-Rashid, although the historical characters are all traceable to the Mamluk period around the 14th century. The four stories in which Ahmad al-Danif and Hasan Shuman make cameo appearances are a good example of the structure, themes, characters, plot, and narrative typical in stories of the *Nights* that deal with the underworld and its shady inhabitants, and the role and status of *muhtalun*, *shuttar* and *'ayyarun*. More important, they provide a blueprint for an interpretation of similar stories, whether within or outside the *Nights*.

These characters all begin their careers as thieves and bandits. In ''Ali Shar and Zumurrud', they seem to lead a band of 40 thieves (*lusus*) who call themselves *shuttar*. They are outlaws, and live in a cave. One of them, Jawan al-Kurdi al-Shatir, kills a solider, puts on his clothes and goes into town to steal. He inadvertently 'kidnaps' Zumurrud and brings her to the cave. He entrusts her to his mother and leaves again for the city to steal. Zumurrud outwits the mother and escapes to a city where she becomes queen. Jawan al-Kurdi happens to pass through her kingdom, and she spots him, has poison put in his food and kills him, exacting her revenge. Ahmad al-Danif and his 'band of brothers' are thieves and bandits, or outlaws, who operate outside the law. As outlaws, they commit crimes and are punished for them.

They then appear in 'Aladdin with Moles on His Cheeks'. Here, they seem to have joined the service of Harun al-Rashid as police lieutenants. Their relationship with Harun al-Rashid and with his system of justice, however, is ambivalent. Aladdin at one time becomes a close companion of Harun al-Rashid and the chief merchant of Baghdad. Later in the story, the son of the governor of Baghdad competes with him for the favours of a slave-girl, Yasamin, and employs a thief who steals Harun al-Rashid's ring (and other things) and plants them in Aladdin's house. When Harun al-Rashid's personal effects are found in Aladdin's house, Aladdin is sentenced to be hanged in the public square.

Ahmad al-Danif, who has previously adopted Aladdin as an honorary son, finds out and secretly rescues him from the gallows by substituting the body of an already executed 'criminal'. Aladdin is of course exonerated at the end and the real culprits are caught and punished. Here, Ahmad al-Danif and Hasan Shuman serve Harun al-Rashid when he is right, but they also do not hesitate to disobey his orders, albeit in secret, when they deem that what he has done was unjust.

In these Arabic stories, Ahmad al-Danif and Hasan Shuman clearly follow a similar career path to the Chinese *haohan* as well as *xiake* in contemporary *wuxia* fiction and *kung fu* movies. They begin as outlaws and when they come into conflict with the corrupt officers of the court, their intelligence, martial skills, sense of justice, and willingness to stick their necks out to help the downtrodden attract the attention of the emperor, and they are recognized and integrated into the imperial court.[8]

Outlaws and Law in Arabic and Chinese Stories

These Arabic and Chinese stories challenge the legitimacy of kinship-based kingship especially when kingship fails to uphold the law. They move the arena of action outside the palace to the streets and outposts. There, they put the government officers under close scrutiny, particularly their violations of the friendship–brotherhood bond. For this bond, as I have mentioned, structures the relationship between sovereign and his officers and subjects, among the officers of the court and their relationship with the subjects they serve. Friendship-brotherhood, as al-Tawhidi would say, applies equally to those who are companions to, and in the service of, the ruler. We see this clearly in the story of Wu Song in *Water Margin* and Dalila in 'Dalila al-Muhtala'.

Haohan in Water Margin

Wu Song is one of the *haohan* outlaws in *Water Margin*. He is handsome, skilled in martial arts and loyal to his brother and friends. He can be impetuous. He becomes famous for slaying a tiger with his bare hands while drunk. He escapes to the distant province of Liangshan after he kills his brother's murderers, his sister-in-law and her lover. He takes matters into his own hands after exhausting all legal means. Bureaucrats and merchants are the villains here. They have no respect for the idea of 'friendship' or 'brotherhood'. They have no scruples when plotting against their family, friends, and colleagues. Like Liu, Guan, and Zhang in *The Three Kingdoms*, who embody the qualities al-Tawhidi ascribes to brotherhood and friendship, 'care, preservation, loyalty, advice, help, generosity and consolation',[9] Wu Song, who is loyal, honest, and just, falls victim to their machinations frequently.

More significantly, 'brotherhood' takes two forms in Wu Song's tale: friendship and family. There is however, no contradiction between them. When his brother dies, 'familial brotherhood' ends, but 'friendship brotherhood' continues. In fact, it remains the only social network to which he belongs. This friendship network slowly narrows down to the outlaws of Liangshan. The 108 *haohan* are united in one cause, to restore justice to the empire. The outlaws become the law enforcers. Ideal brotherhood gives law its legitimacy. In its absence among officers of the law, their law becomes suspect.

Shatir in Dalila al-Muhtala

This sense of justice, as located outside the machinery of rule, is familiar in the Arabic stories of Dalila al-Muhtala, ʿAli al-Zaybaq, Hasan Shuman and Ahmad al-Danif. When the officers of the court are incompetent or corrupt, these *shuttar* form their own network of power and sprint into action. They live with friends who serve as their network of power. More importantly, the government officers lose their credibility (and legitimacy) when they are oblivious or turn a blind eye to violations of the law, while the *shuttar* can take law into their own hands when they are right and just.

Dalila is the widow of a police captain. However, as a woman, she is not allowed to inherit her husband's job or pension and must live in poverty, even though she is equally clever and skilled in martial arts. Worse, Hasan Shuman and Ahmad al-Danif, who were originally outlaws, now occupy her husband's posts. In a moment of indignation, she goes out into the streets of Baghdad, plays con tricks on its citizens, from the porters and shopkeepers to the chief judge and governor. Her doings attract the attention of Harun al-Rashid, who steps in to right the wrong done to her. He awards her husband's pension to her, appoints her the keeper of both his postal pigeons and the guest house he has established for itinerant merchants.

Such stories are universal. *The Lord of the Rings* and *Harry Potter* are contemporary examples. Sauron and Voldemort are more like Cao Cao than Harun al-Rashid. They are modern tyrants. Neither is interested in peace, fairness, or harmony among their officers and subjects. They impose their rule by striking fear in their officers and persecuting their subjects. Their officers, in turn, are instruments of tyranny not justice. Those wronged or harmed and relatives of those killed in the process have no recourse to any form of redress. Law becomes synonymous with lawlessness when it fails to ensure communal harmony or uphold the principles of doing what is right and righting wrongs.

Under such circumstances, when justice is perverted by the machinery of power, the sovereign, his officers, and even his subjects, then rebellion for the purpose of restoring just rule and reenabling law that underpins justice is most welcome. We root for Frodo, Aragorn, and the fellowship of the ring, and Harry, Hermione, Ron, and their friends and allies, when they go all out after Sauron and Voldemort, and we rejoice in their eventual triumph, for with their success harmony returns to community, as does justice.

Love and Passion in Just Rule

However, ideal brotherhood or friendship alone, as we shall see, is not sufficient foundation for a harmonious community. It can place the brothers or friends outside the community and remove law from rule. For a community to recover from lawlessness, law must be reintegrated into rule, and the outlaws must be reintegrated into the rule of the community, for ideal brotherhood is most potent when it serves both law and rule. More importantly, the ruler must attend to justice and run the affairs of the state in person.

This comes across clearly in Arabic and Chinese stories, as well as in *The Lord of the Rings*. Distraction on the part of Harun al-Rashid in 'Aladdin with Moles on His Cheeks', Emperor Huizong (r. 1100-1126) of the Song Dynasty (960-1279) in *Water Margin*, and Aragorn in *The Lord of the Rings*, allows injustice to take place, or their officers to be unjust, and they alone can restore justice to its rightful place when violations occur. Harun al-Rashid recruits the *shuttar* into his service as police lieutenants. Song Huizong conscripts the 108 *haohan* into his army when he learns of their plight, and they go on to fight for his empire. And Aragorn assumes his role as king of Middle Earth.

Inherent in the discourses on friendship and brotherhood is yet another discourse on the ruler and his legitimacy. It prescribes a rather strict regime for the ruler, which he must follow to the letter. We see this clearly in the development of the character of Song Jiang in *Water Margin*. On the surface, the novel, just like the stories of the *shuttar*, *'ayyarun* and *muhtalun* stories in Arabic, seems to assert the potential of friendship in underpinning just rule in an ideal community so long as the ruler combines wisdom with action, as implied in al-Tawhidi's discourse on *al-sadaqa and al-sadiq*.

However, the transformation of Song Jiang from hero to tyrant reveals the contradiction between friendship brotherhood and family brotherhood and, more significantly, demonstrates that friendship alone, whether inside or outside the family, is insufficient to build and sustain empire, community or society. In the Chinese context, it is only one of the five principal relationships underpinning the fabric of society, and in the Arabic context, it cannot replace ideal love as the paradigm for the coherence of community.

The story of Song Jiang, a small government officer turned leader of the 108 *haohan* and king of Liangshan, is marked by the absence of harmony in four social relationships. His liaison with a manipulative woman results in him killing her, his involvement with the Lianghsan *haohan* distracts him from his duties towards his father and brother, and his rebellion against Emperor Huizong violates his loyalty to his king.

The absence of ideal love in Song's life in particular, and *Water Margin* in general, is symptomatic of the incompleteness or imperfection of the Liangshan community. The conflict of friendship with filial duty, *xiao*, required of him as a son towards his father, with the duty of care in brotherhood towards his flesh-and-blood brother, and with loyalty to the sovereign, *zhong*, he, as officer, owes his ruler, are all ominous signs. In his failures to look after his father and brother and to serve his emperor, he grows increasingly foolish. His actions become so dictated by his passion that in the end he even fails his friends and forfeits his loyalty to them, *yi*.[10]

This brings us back squarely to the dialectics between love and desire, or reason and passion, and to al-Tawhidi. Friendship, in the examples we see from Arabic and Chinese storytelling, is often founded on a kind of passionate love, *hawa*, just like male-female love, and it often conflicts with reason, *'aql*, which must necessarily be the foundation of the ideal community, such as al-Farabi's *al-madina al-fadila*; when reason is disabled, this ideal community turns into a sin city, *al-madina al-fasiqa*. Reason, *'aql* in Arabic or *li* in Chinese, is indispensable in a man's conduct, and it must govern his relationship, as ruler, with his officers and subjects including slaves, as a father with his children, as a brother with his siblings, and as a husband with his wives. This code of conduct is applicable equally to the ruler and to the officers of the court, especially the viziers, and the members of the community, merchants, and labourers alike in the world of the Solomon legends and the Harun al-Rashid myths we have already seen.

Chapter 5

Joie de Vivre: Life is a Banquet

Don't you see,
The Water of Yellow River
   From the Heaven is brought –
To the sea it rushes and returns not?

Don't you see,
By the mirror over their white hair
   our parents grieve –
It's like black silk in the morn but snow at
   eve.

Make merry to the full
   when life wishes are granted;
Under the moon,
   Gold jugs unattended one mustn't leave.
            Li Bai (701–795), *Tang Poems*

Living properly and enjoying life are not mutually exclusive. Arabic stories, whether in the
form of *akhbar* (anecdotes), *hikayat* (tales), or
qisas (stories) in *adab* collections, Arabic
epics, the *Nights*, or *Tales of the Marvellous and
News of the Strange*, may begin with too much
pleasure and too little work, but always end with
re-establishing an equilibrium between propriety

and *joie de vivre*. Banquets of delicate dishes and fine wines, musical concerts, and storytelling assemblies are staples of Arabic stories. Food and story can be the catalyst for adventures and storytelling and above all discoveries of injustices and righting wrongs. Story is the journey of discovery of the self through the world that pulls the protagonist out from ignorance into knowledge, and from wandering back into a good life.

Frodo, Aragorn, and Harry Potter learn about themselves in their encounters with living beings from all walks of life as well as in challenging situations. Normal life returns as soon as they complete their journeys. They resume the *joie de vivre* drawn from the mundanity of the quotidian. The poet Li Bai calls upon us to enjoy life to the full, to drink, eat and be merry, especially when life is full of unpredictable toils and, of course, death. In Arabic storytelling, 'The Seven Voyages of Sindbad the Sailor' and 'Hasib Karim al-Din' are two famous examples.

Sindbad and Hasib Karim al-Din, both left fatherless at a young age and bequeathed large fortunes but recalcitrant to their mothers' education, lose everything and must earn back their fortunes after a series of misadventures. When relief arrives after hardship, both protagonists have learned their lessons and matured into responsible human beings. Each inherits his father's vocation, with Sindbad now a rich merchant and Hasib Karim al-Din a vizier. 'The Seven Voyages of Sindbad the Sailor'

Figure 21. Still from the 1974 animated film *Sindbad* (1974, Karel Zeman) from Czechoslovakia.

interestingly does not end on this happy note. There is an epilogue to Sindbad's adventures. He holds a social gathering at his palatial home every night, offers his guests a lavish banquet, and exchanges stories with them.

One night, Sindbad the Porter stumbles into Sindbad the Sailor's garden in despair and is invited to join the party. At the end of the evening, having heard the story of one of the sailor's voyages, the porter receives a gift of a hundred gold dinars. Seven nights, seven stories, and seven gifts later, Sindbad the Porter is seven hundred dinars richer and has been given the means of a respectable life. Such an ending is never gratuitous, as we shall see in the next chapter, for listening, not just hearing, is an important aspect of Arabic storytelling. Contemplation on the meaning of life often ensues.

Figure 22. Sindbad the Sailor receiving Sindbad the Porter, illustration for 'Sindbad the Sailor', from *The Arabian Nights*, 1895 (colour engraving) (French School).

This said, Sindbad the porter is rewarded for enjoying both the banquet and the stories.

Joie de Vivre, Material and Literary

Joie de vivre comes in material and literary forms. These two forms come to be intertwined in Arabic storytelling. As food, wine, music, and story are conveyed in word, the story takes the form of a literary banquet in which play with word becomes synonymous with play at a banquet where food and wine are served, music is performed, and stories are told.

The story world, like Barbieland in the 2023 film *Barbie*, is a refraction of the real world. Story is like Barbie, imagined and created as a foil of the flesh-and-blood woman. Her beauty is perfect and so is life in Barbieland. Nothing disturbs or tarnishes the happy-go-lucky bliss there. Barbie and her Barbieland are of course the effect of storytelling, and they exist only in a story world. Its fictionality is driven home when it is brought into contact with the real world. As Ruth Handler, the original maker of the doll, tells the stereotypical Barbie, a blonde girl with a perfectly shaped physique, she created Barbie and Barbieland because being human is hard and living in the real world is even harder. Arabic storytelling is all too aware of the tension between the ideal world and the real world, the paradigmatic code of conduct and its application. It never hesitates to mock and unravel the very world of perfect beauty it constructs.

Figure 23. Barbie (Margot Robbie) meets her creator, Ruth Handler (Rhea Perlman), in *Barbie* (dir. Greta Gerwig, 2023).

Beauty in the *Thousand and One Nights* is physical, but this physical beauty is a sign of a more important kind of beauty, that of words and deeds, of speech and conduct, or more aptly, moral beauty. Moral beauty comes in the form of physical perfection. The ideal pair in the *Nights* love stories is one manifestation. The pair are matched in perfect beauty and propriety in their behaviour in love. Their devotion to each other is such that they resist all temptations thrown in their path until they are united in marriage. Words and deeds are inextricably connected in the *Nights*. Stories result in action and in justice, particularly morally beautiful stories of fidelity in love and loyalty among the power elite and members of an ideal community. The reward for good words and deeds comes in the form of recognition and a life of comfort and happiness. The opposite solicits punishment, it goes without saying.

'The Hunchback', including the cycle of eleven tales within it, and 'The Two Viziers' take us into a world that is not perfect. The story complicates the discourse by disrupting the symmetry of the physical, verbal and behavioural beauty underpinning the *Nights*. Love stories slip from the familiar pattern of perfect love into imperfection then farce. 'The Hunchback' and 'The Two Viziers' mirror, interrogate, and challenge the Solomon legends, the Harun al-Rashid myths and *adab* as both a practice and a cultural institution. Focalizing the stories on the idea of distraction, *fitna*, the stories told within 'The Hunchback' and 'The Two Viziers' make a mockery of the patronage system, idealized as the mechanism of appropriate reward for beautiful words, in this case for storytelling itself, and questioning the very value of words and the efficacy of storytelling. They take pleasure in making fun of the ideal world they themselves construct.

The Hunchback

The satire takes the form of a literary banquet in 'The Hunchback'. Humour, dark and cruel, is derived from the mirth the characters in the story experience from the misadventures of the misshapen body of the hunchback as he is paraded and abused publicly. The hunchback is a stock character of humorous narrative in the *Nights*, '[whose] physical deformity [...] enhances the tale's jocular potential'.[1] The story begins tantalizingly with an evening out enjoying food, wine and entertainment, but ends with a storytelling assembly before the sovereign, court officers, and practically everyone in the community.

> It is related, O King, that there lived once in China a tailor who had a pretty, compatible, and loyal wife. It happened one day that they went out for a stroll to enjoy the sights at a place of entertainment, where they spent the whole day in diversions and fun, and when they returned home at the end of the day, they met on the way a jolly hunchback. He was smartly dressed in a folded inner robe and an open outer robe, with gathered sleeves and an embroidered collarband, in the Egyptian style, and sporting a scarf and tall green hat, with knots of yellow silk stuffed with ambergris. The hunchback was short, like him of whom the poet 'Antar said:
>
> > Lovely the hunchback who can hide his hump,
> > Like a pearl hidden in an oyster shell,
> > A man who looks like a castor oil branch,
> > From which dangles a rotten citric lump.
>
> He was busy playing on the tambourine, singing, and improvising all kinds of funny gestures. When they drew near and looked

at him, they saw he was drunk, reeking of wine.

[. . .]

[T]hey were delighted with him and invited him home to sup and drink with them that night. He accepted gladly and walked with them to their home.[2]

If the title of the story implies that the hunchback will be the protagonist of this story, that expectation is soon dashed. After the hunchback makes the mistake of accepting the tailor and his wife's invitation to dinner and a night of fun, he chokes on a bone hidden in the morsel of fish that the tailor crams into his mouth and he dies.

He remains dead until the very end of the eleven stories contained in 'The Hunchback', when the morsel of fish is removed from his throat, and he comes back to life. For the entire duration, the hunchback is nothing more than a corpse that is passed on from the tailor to a Jewish physician, a steward, and at last a Christian broker, who is caught red-handed by the police, and all end up before the governor, who begins murder trials. He is finally returned to the King of China, his true master, when the King hears of the multiple confessions to the murder of his favourite companion, and comes to preside over the trials.

The hunchback is oblivious to the trials for his murder, which are taking place right before him, and deaf to all the stories his purported murderers tell to save each other's lives. In these stories, the protagonists lose body parts after they follow desire which leads to their committing some crime or infringement. A prattling barber then intrudes on the scene and tells seven stories of how he and his six brothers all suffer abuse and lose bits and pieces of their bodies, as well as their livelihoods, through no fault of their own. The hunchback only wakes up at the very end of the cycle, when the barber 'drew out the piece of fish with the bone, soaked in blood. Suddenly the hunchback sneezed and stood up, rubbing his face with his hand'.[3]

The Two Viziers

The hunchback in 'The Two Viziers' is similarly the site of practical jokes. Here, he is in the service of the Sultan of Egypt, who gets angry when he is refused as a match for his vizier's daughter, Sitt al-Husn, and decides to punish them by marrying her to the ugliest of his servants, who even when 'wearing a brocaded robe of honor and a double turban', looks 'with his neck buried between his shoulders, sat rolled up like a ball, [...] more like a toy than a man'.[4] Unfortunately for the hunchback, a pair of naughty demons intervene to settle a bet on whether Sitt al-Husn or Badr al-Din is more beautiful. They decide to bring Badr al-Din from Basra to Sitt al-Husn in Cairo. They do and place him side by side with the hunchback before the bride throughout the wedding procession.

The hunchback in both stories is the recipient of physical manipulation, from being a lifeless corpse being carried around to a bulk of awkward flesh getting hung upside down, and as such his body is the site of scatological pranks. He has no presence and is always silent. His silent presence is a reminder that something is afoot in each story, and that together they – the two stories – make an even stronger statement. His ugliness accentuates the beauty of Sitt al-Husn and Badr al-Din in 'The Two Viziers'; his dead silence in 'The Hunchback' highlights the buoyant prattle of the barber and, more importantly, his absurdity, whether in his appearance, behavior, thinking, or situation, echoes the absurd situation in which all the protagonists of the story find themselves.

Satire of Adab

This absurd situation, which differs greatly in detail between the two stories, follows a trajectory of escalation, from the 'The Two Viziers' to 'The Hunchback', and ends in a satire that parodies the moral universe that the *Nights* stories construct. This satire relies on dehumanizing the hunchback, on depriving him of both his voice and his role as the court clown. His silence and inaction make it possible to show how storytelling can trip on the tongue of the teller, twist the narrative around its own neck, turn purposeful story into prattle, unravel discourse as conceit, and render language powerless.

More significantly, these stories make fun of an economy of exchange based in language. These two stories, despite their indulgence in cruel treatment of, and laughter derived from, the disfigured body, are two faces of a discourse on the ambivalence about the power of language, that it brings riches and saves life. They interrogate the fundamental faith in the performativity of language, that language is both action and impact. The hunchback is a code in a word game. The ugliness and imperfect body of the hunchback are the opposites of the beauty and physical perfection of heroes and heroines in the *Nights* stories. 'The Hunchback' makes fun of stories like 'The Two Viziers', which is itself a literary conceit.

'The Hunchback' is in part rhymed prose and in another part poetry. Its narrative is generated through two of the most important rhetorical devices in classical Arabic *adab* – doubling and opposition – and two of the most intriguing morphological mechanisms for generating words and meanings in the Arabic language – paradoxes and derivation. Characters come in pairs, even twins: the two viziers, Shams al-Din and Nur al-Din, their wives, and their children, Sitt al-Husn and Badr al-Din, and the two demons, who are almost mirror images of each other. Either they begin together in the same place in the story then diverge, such as Shams al-Din and Nur al-Din; or they begin in different places then converge, such as Sitt al-Husn and Badr al-Din, or the two demons.

Sitt al-Husn and Badr al-Din follow yet another itinerary of divergence and convergence. This doubling generates characters and moves the story along parallel lines: Shams al-Din remains in Cairo, gets married and has a daughter, Sitt al-Husn, and Nur al-Din, goes to Basra, marries there and has a son, Badr al-Din, generating more stories. These doubles are juxtaposed to unique characters, particularly ʿAjib and the hunchback, which serve as convergence knots for the diverging story lines.

The pairs bask in physical and moral beauty. Shams al-Din and Nur al-Din, sons of a 'wise, experienced, and influential vizier',[5] are described as 'two moons or two lovely deer in their perfect elegance, beauty, and grace'[6] and Badr al-Din at birth as having 'a figure as slender as a bough, was endowed by God with beauty, charm and prefect grace, so that he captured the heart with his loveliness and captivated the mind with his perfection. He was so faultless in character and looks that the deer stole from him their necks and eyes and every other grace',[7] and when grown up (in the words of the he-demon), 'This can be none other than one of the children of Paradise, whom God has created to tempt all mortals'.[8]

His counterpart, Sitt al-Husn, according to the she-demon, 'bears the most striking resemblance to this young man, for with an elegant and fine figure, she is endowed with beauty, charm, and perfect grace'.[9] ʿAjib, the singular descendant of this line of 'beauty, charm and grace', has 'a face as round as the full moon or the rising sun, a radiant brow, and rosy cheeks'.[10] Their beauty is juxtaposed to the ugliness of the hunchback, best conveyed in the following comparison between him and Badr al-Din on Sitt al-Husn's wedding night:

> When the women saw Hasan al-Basri's beauty and grace and looked on his face, which was as bright as the new moon and as dazzling as the full moon, and looked on his body, which swayed like a willow bough, they loved his charm and flirtatious looks, and when he showered them with money, they loved him even more. They crowded around him with their lighted candles and gazed on his beauty and envied him his charm, winking at each other, for everyone said, 'None deserves our bride but this young man. What a pity to waste her on the worthless hunchback! May God curse him who brought this about!' and they cursed the king. [...] Then the women began to curse the hunchback and to jeer at him, while they prayed for Badr al-Din Hasan and ingratiated themselves with him.[11]

Here, the hunchback is linked to the pair of kings, the king of Cairo and the king of Basra, who also serve as narrative convergence knots: the king of Cairo, having been denied the hand of Sitt al-Husn, decides to marry her to the hunchback, and puts the hunchback at the centre stage of the wedding ceremony; the king of Basra, having been angered by Badr al-Din's two-month long mourning after his father's death, dismisses him from his post as vizier, confiscates all his properties, and causes him to run for his life, resulting in his being carried by the two demons to wed his cousin in Cairo. The hunchback is an ugly sign in a story of beautiful people divided then united, disturbing the symmetry of a literary text intricately composed from the doubling of characters and narratives, and from their movements in parallel and opposite directions.

Beauty and Distraction

The hunchback is the distraction, *fitna*, in the text, a discord, dissonance, or temptation designed to distract us from the lure of beauty, here created in language, and to look at its opposite, at ugliness, which in turn draws our attention to the two kings, and more particularly, to their quick anger and rash behaviour, or passion. Which good king would force himself on his vizier's young daughter and when refused impose on her an ugly hunchback for a husband? And which king would fire his vizier mourning a beloved father? But are the two kings the true culprits in the story? Are not the two viziers, our titular protagonists, the victims of similar hot temper and irrational conduct?

When Nur al-Din tells his father-in-law, the old vizier to the King of Basra, who he is and his reason for leaving his hometown Cairo, the vizier says with a smile, 'My son, you quarreled even before getting married and having children!'[12] Indeed. The source of the brothers' quarrel is nothing more than fantasies exchanged in words, of words said in jest, as we saw in the preceding chapter. The talk of marrying their son and daughter to each other leads to teasing about dowry, and this teasing turns into a quarrel about which unborn child is worthier, the daughter of the older brother or the son of the younger. Similarly, the union between Sitt al-Husn and Badr al-Din is brought about by the two demons trying to settle a squabble about which of them is more beautiful. Words uttered even in jest, this story seems to say, can have an irreversible impact on people and their fate.

Here, words are on the contrary, *fitna*, dissonance, distraction, and discord, not solution or resolution. We see this in Badr al-Din, the seeming opposite of the hunchback, who is similarly described as *fitna*. For all his perfection, physical beauty and literary arts in one package, Badr al-Din may inspire beautiful prose and poetry, or literary feats that rival *adab*, but, like the hunchback, he lacks mastery of, and in, his own life. He is a chess piece in a game of fate, a body that is moved around arbitrarily, in his case from Basra to Cairo and Damascus, just like the hunchback's corpse in 'The Hunchback', and a man utterly helpless despite all his literary pretensions and intellectual qualifications.

Badr al-Din ends up in Damascus as a cook at a reformed robber's shop, and is lost to his wife and son, ʿAjib, for ten or twelve years. Even when his uncle Shams al-Din initiates a search, Badr al-Din cannot be found. In the very end, a sweet dish he makes based on his mother's recipe, 'a sizzling bowl of pomegranate seeds conserved with almonds and sugar',[13] saves the day.

On their way to Basra, the search party passes through Damascus, and ʿAjib, being the irrepressible youth that he is, goes out to the streets to play. He encounters his father, unbeknownst to him, and has a taste of this singular dish. Father and son feel an instinctive tenderness for one another, but these pangs of recognition do not lead to reunion but rather to misunderstanding. When Badr al-Din follows ʿAjib back to camp, ʿAjib suspects his father is a paedophile, throws a rock at Badr al-Din's head and scars him. There go his good looks!

However, on their way back from Basra, having reunited with Badr al-Din's mother, ʿAjib cannot help his longing for Badr al-Din and goes to his shop one more time. His father feeds him another 'pomegranate-seeds dish, preserved in almonds and sweet julep and flavored with cardamom and rosewater'.[14] ʿAjib returns to camp to find his newfound grandmother having made the same 'pomegranate-seed dish, except that this one has less sugar'. He takes a bite and rejects it as inferior to what he has just eaten in the street. But no one knows how to make this dish better than I but my son Badr al-Din, his grandmother exclaims!

The rest should be history, but not in this instance, for a final trick has yet to be played out. To make sure he is truly Sitt al-Husn's husband and 'Ajib's father, Shams al-Din sets another trap for Badr al-Din. He orders him to deliver the same dish to his camp, but has him captured, or rather abducted, and taken to Cairo on the pretext that Badr al-Din had cheated on the ingredients; the dish contained too little pepper. There, his earlier wedding night is recreated and when everything is ready, he is brought out of his incarceration and reunited with first his wife and later the entire family.

Word and Food

Two means make reunion happen in this story: 'Ajib and the pomegranate-seed dish. 'Ajib may look like his parents, having 'a face as round as the full moon or the rising sun, a radiant brow, and rosy cheeks',[15] 'all beauty, charm and perfect grace',[16] and of 'extraordinary beauty and grace',[17] but he is no pushover. In fact, he 'began to bully, beat and abuse the other children'[18] at the tender age of ten. He is not the mirror image of his parents, or grandfather and great uncle.

If Badr al-Din is given 'good education' and 'taught good manners' at the age of seven,[19] and 'learned to read and write the Arabic language, as well as calligraphy, mathematics, and jurisprudence' at the age of twelve, 'Ajib does not seem to have learned even the lessons on good manners.[20] If Badr al-Din seems to abide by the advice his father gave him on his death bed: to associate with no one, to oppress no one, to hold his tongue and preserve silence, to avoid alcohol, and to protect his wealth, 'Ajib violates at least

Figure 24. The Wedding Banquet, *Maqamat al-Hariri* by al-Hariri of Basra (d. 1122), c. 1225–1235.

three of these five principles (alcohol is irrelevant in the story, and he is too young to worry about wealth).

'Ajib may be his father's mirror image in physical beauty, but he is really the king's double in his 'oppressive' inclinations. He may never break out into poetry as his parents constantly do, but he makes demands and takes action. If poetry veils the silence and stillness of the other characters, placing action in interior emotion, his silence on poetry puts him in the arena of action, in exteriority. This little terror, the third '*fitna*' in the story, who goes out into streets 'followed by a eunuch carrying a red club of knotted almond wood', 'with which if one hits a camel, it would go galloping as far as Yemen',[21] and gathers a huge admiring crowd around him, is the catalyst for the eventual family reunion.

Word, the story seems to suggest, can be 'distraction' as we have seen, but it is also akin to silence, and we see this in the literary arts, particularly poetry, where emotive expressions rarely lead to deeds. 'The Hunchback' raises questions about the efficacy of storytelling. Can the stories Shahrazad tells Shahriyar educate his passion into love? Word is powerless in more ways than one. That word is simultaneously voice and silence, power and powerlessness, or performative and inactive, is another playing out of a feature of a group of Arabic words known as *addad*. In each of these, a word contains a meaning and its opposite simultaneously. Silence, like such words, is paradoxical. It can save life, just like storytelling.

The interplay between silence as action and voice as distraction, here, in relation to word, parallels that of powerlessness and power in the story Ja'far tells Harun al-Rashid, 'The Two Viziers', or for that matter, his attitude and conduct in the story of 'The Three Apples', in which his silent endurance seems more effective than action, and more productive than telling stories to save life. Silence frees the individual to act. The two characters who act or do things in 'The Two Viziers' are servants (eunuchs) and children ('Ajib). They are not educated in *adab*. Likewise, none of the stories told to the king of China in 'The Hunchback' to save life succeeds, but the practical skill of a barber well versed in medicine saves not only the hunchback but all the protagonists on trial for his murder. These figures move the arena of action from word to food and, more importantly, from literary arts to practical skills.

Food and Action

Food is a multilayered code of both pragmatism and wordplay. The pomegranate-seed dish plays a key role in the development of the narrative plot of 'The Two Viziers'. It is at once the means, mechanism and site of recognition and reunion. The plot is woven and resolved around this dish. It is, as we have seen, Badr al-Din's heirloom, his identity marker, and in the final analysis his salvation. The morsel of fish in 'The Hunchback' plays a similar role in the resolution of the story. The story begins and ends with it. Eating it kills the hunchback, and its removal from his throat brings him back to life.

If the removal of the arena of action from word to food, and from the literary arts to practical skills, is the ultimate joke in a text with literary pretensions, the morsel of fish partakes in a word game that is quite different from that of the pomegranate-seed dish. It straddles two types of stories: stories intended to save life and stories intended to be funny. But these two types of stories are not mutually exclusive. The king of China in 'The Hunchback' may prefer the barber's funny stories to those intended to save life, but Harun al-Rashid remains a fan of communal harmony in his understanding of 'The Two Viziers'. Just as the king of China finds the barber's stories 'more marvellous and wondrous', Harun al-Rashid describes 'The Two Viziers' as the 'wonder of wonders'. However, the moral associated with storytelling of the *Thousand and One Nights* is intact. There is no death-caused-by-betrayal in 'The Hunchback' or 'The Two Viziers', therefore, no life to save or death to postpone.

*　　*　　*

Stories about all aspects of humanity are welcome. These hunchback stories, told alongside other Solomon legends and the Harun al-Rashid myths in the *Nights* and *Tales of the Marvellous and News of the Strange*, are a humorous reminder of the ugly side of humanity and that the story world is fiction even though its inherent ideal community is carved out of the real world. A story worth telling is one that brings to the fore the dialogue between the two worlds leading to the transformation of both. The cruelty of the flesh-and-blood human beings may be educated into kindness, and the ugliness of the real world can be reshaped into beauty.[22]

The encounter between Barbieland and the real world shows this. The Barbies may reflect the diversity of women, their increasing presence in the professions, and their growing power in the real world, but the real world, as the stereotypical Barbie herself witnesses, is still ruled by men and full of injustice and struggle. Equally, the female-centered Barbieland marginalizes the Kens, and leaves men unhappy and ready to revolt, especially after they hear the stereotypical Ken's accounts of how well men fare in the male-centered real world. The stereotypical Barbie and Ken visit the real world, and the men and women from Mattel, the company that made Barbie, come to Barbieland, with all working out what may be improved in their respective worlds. There will always be stories to tell, for perfection remains out of reach.

Chapter 6

Heaven on Earth: Storytelling and Meanings of Life

'I learned too, Your Majesty,' said Sindbad, 'that man may be afforded a miracle, but it is not sufficient that he should use it and appropriate it; he must also approach it with guidance from the light of God that shines in his heart'.

Naguib Mahfouz, *Arabian Nights and Days*[1]

In Naguib Mahfouz's 1979 rewriting of the *Thousand and One Nights, Arabian Nights and Days*, Sindbad the Sailor is summoned to Shahriyar's court towards the end of the novel. The repentant Shahriyar in Mahfouz's political allegory has now abdicated his throne and handed over the running of the state to three members of the community who have proven incorruptible. Marouf the Cobbler, Aladdin with Moles on His Cheeks, and Abdallah the Sage, having successfully resisted the allure of power given to them in the form of Solomon's magical objects – the hat of invisibility, flying carpet and magical ring – are now judged fit to rule. All is well. The community is transforming itself into an ideal community.[2]

Shahriyar should be content and proud, but he remains despondent. When he hears of Sindbad's return, he is curious to know the lessons Sindbad learned from his adventures that transformed him from the youth he was into the wise man he has become: 'You have seen such wonders of the world as no human eye has seen, and you have learned many lessons, so rejoice in what God has bestowed upon you in the way of wealth and wisdom'.[3]

The stories Sindbad tells, and the lessons he summarizes, send Shahriyar on his own journey in search of the meaning of life. In his enlightened state, having heard one thousand and one nights' worth of stories from Shahrazad, Shahriyar yearns not for worldly power – food, traditions, and occasional miracles – but for what is beyond this world and this life. He is intrigued by the lesson that Sindbad learned out at sea, that 'freedom is the life of the spirit and Paradise itself is of no avail to man if he has lost his freedom'.[4]

Shahriyar may have made it possible for an ideal community to begin to take shape, but is this the only purpose of his life? How can he know if he has never embarked on the kind of adventures Sindbad has experienced? He has yet to leave the confinement of his palace and kingdom. He may have been touring around the kingdom he rules over at night, Harun al-Rashid-like, but has yet to experience the wonders he has heard about first-hand. Is the paradise on earth he brings into existence not a prison-house that stands in the way of his freedom, and hence in the way of enlightenment and spirituality?

Meaning through Paradox

The imagined ideal community, utopia, is necessarily totalitarian, tyrannical, and oppressive because absolute order must be maintained at all costs. There is no room for desire because that is charged with transgressive impulses and wanderlust. Desire must necessarily be educated and fitted into the utopian straitjacket. With the domestication of desire, utopia closes in on itself, and in its isolation it becomes, so to speak, frozen in time and place. In other words, there is no life in utopia: everyone must live a regimented life like a robot. There can be no curiosity, no wonder, and no wandering, without which new knowledge may not be created. But if desire frees itself of the straitjacket, comes back to life and disturbs the order of things, the world changes into dystopia. When this happens, another quest is necessary, and a new adventure begins.

The Lord of the Rings follows the 'history repeats itself' trajectory framed by a harmonious past disrupted by a tyrant craving world domination and a present that sees the triumphant return of love. Desire and love come in one package. Without desire there is no love. Adventures are journeys into the complex world of desire and love, and a balancing act between keeping anarchy at bay and allowing life to thrive. 'Sindbad the Sailor' expresses this paradox best.

Sindbad, whether in the *Nights* or Mahfouz's rewriting, epitomizes the role of desire in every human being's journey of discovery. This journey is both internal and external. Sindbad the porter in the *Nights* represents the world within and Sindbad the sailor the immensity of what is out there to be explored. The fantastic world and beings these stories inherit from the Solomon legends tell us that life is more than the material conditions of human living, such as acquiring wealth and power, making family, enjoying food and drink, or even building an ideal community on earth. They offer us a glimpse of an infinite pluriverse that is beyond human comprehension.

Solomon's traces, the fantastic beings, the sea world, and transmogrification serve as a reminder of the limits of human knowledge acquired through lived experience. Both the lived experience and the attendant knowledge can barely scratch the surface of what is out there in the infinite pluriverse. Whereas the Harun al-Rashid myths concern themselves with the ideal community underpinned by a moral universe structured around beauty and led by an iconized just ruler, the Solomon legends question and challenge their inherent ontology and epistemology.

Solomon's once fabulous kingdom and riches are also a reminder of the transience of life on earth. Death marks the end of Solomon's life in *qisas al-anbiya'* but the beginning of his afterlife in the *Nights*. The macabre feel of the Solomon legends in the *Nights*, as juxtaposed to the triumphant tone in *Tales of the Prophets* – prophets are always victorious – masks an optimism that is apprehended only by those who can see beyond the immediacy of wealth and power, kingdom and kingship. Paradoxically, the rather loud celebration of the lives of the prophets in the *Tales of the Prophets* cannot suppress the tangible desire for this-worldly wealth and power. Even at its most pious in the *Tales*, prophecy always seems to be a gift from God that comes wrapped in material wealth and political authority. Solomon's reward for his repentance is the return of his ring and his reinstatement as king.

However, the Solomon legends at the same time interrogate the limits of the ideal community imagined in Arabic storytelling, as we have seen in 'The Merchant and the Genie', 'The Fisherman and the Demon', 'Jullanar', and 'Sindbad the Sailor', and as we shall see in ''Abdallah the Seaman and 'Abdallah the Landman' and 'Hasib Karim al-Din'. In these stories, the world of the sea, hitherto associated with anarchy, serves as the foil for the land-based ideal community. The collision and collusion of the two worlds highlights the symbiosis between desire and love. Yet the relationship between them is more ambivalent than the happy endings of the stories would have us believe.

'Abdallah the Seaman and 'Abdallah the Landman

In ''Abdallah the Seaman and 'Abdallah the Landman', the sea is in fact the source of grace. The landman is a poor fisherman who must live on the generosity of another 'Abdallah, the baker, until he captures the seaman, who in exchange for earthly fruits and nuts brings the landman pearls, corals, and other jewels from the sea. The landman's sudden riches attract suspicion and he is accused of thievery. The king, however, does the right thing, finds out the truth and rewards the landman by making him his son-in-law (notwithstanding his wife and ten children) and right-hand vizier (notwithstanding his lack of qualifications). When the king finds out what a loyal friend the baker has been, the latter too is adopted by the palace and becomes the left-hand vizier. Kingship is working, it seems, and the land is a good world to be on.

There is, however, something unsettlingly mercenary about the king's encouragement of the landman's weekly rendezvous with the seaman. The palace, it seems, would do anything to secure the sea's treasures, even emptying its pantries of food. There is a hint that the prosperity of the kingdom is, after all, dependent on the gifts from the sea and that greed, a desire for worldly goods, has gone slightly out of control. But perhaps the more devastating blow to this utopia is the implicit rejection of the ideology underpinning it. ʿAbdallah the Seaman eventually rejects the world of ʿAbdallah the Landman upon hearing that Muslims on dry land mourn their dead. The ideal community on land that the seaman yearns to hear about and see – the world of Islam – has, according to him, completely misunderstood Islam. The tables are at last turned on the land. The land is for a change the sea's ignorant city, as al-Farabi would say.

The hint here of disillusion with the ideal community and its underpinning ideology – an extra-ordinary interpretation of Islam – remains only a tantalizing clue. While the kingdom's appetite for the riches of the sea is insatiable, there is no hint of desire gone mad or justice undone. The story leaves us in the lurch. We suddenly find ourselves abandoned because our guide, the seaman, is an eccentric who decides to walk out of the story in a huff. This bizarre ending should generate questions in need of answers. What is so outrageous about mourning the dead? There is nothing un-Islamic about it. What is wrong with the world of the land? What makes the sea, on occasion, a better world to be in? The *Nights* may be silent on the subject, but pre-modern Chinese fiction is not. Perhaps what is found in Chinese stories may help to fill a lacuna left by the *Nights* in our understanding of how love and desire function in narrative, informed by the ways in which they construct utopia and dystopia.[5]

Happiness in Community and Individual Fulfilment

The world of Chinese fiction, as we have already seen, is not very different from that of the *Nights*, even though the expressions may seem divergent. Its use of desire as a literary trope through which the symbolic order is established and questioned, as in the *Nights*, is universal.

Pre-modern Chinese fiction has been more fortunate than its Arabic counterpart in that there is a longer tradition of history and commentary that makes it easier for curious readers to contextualize it and grasp its entanglement with the broader Chinese worldview(s). That classical Chinese fiction is political, participating in the ideological contests involving Confucianism, Buddhism, and Daoism is not in dispute. There is, however, a general consensus that a story, short or long, is framed by a meta-narrative articulated in the form of ideal community structured by Confucian ethics.

The sovereign is expected to rule benevolently and justly, righting wrong and punishing evil. His subjects are expected to serve him and the community loyally. However, one is only entitled to serve the sovereign if one succeeds in the civil service examination. Service in turn guarantees the civil servant's, as well as his family's, high social status and prosperity in the world. Loyalty, moreover, extends from sovereign to parents, teachers, friends, colleagues, and underlings. Sexuality is similarly tightly controlled. The Confucian world is located in the material conditions of this life and this world. Buddhism brings to this setup a before- and after-life and a cycle of ongoing rebirths, as well as principles of *karma* and consequence across generations.

More importantly, it situates the Middle Kingdom, the Chinese world, within a world beyond the here and now overseen by the

Buddha. Daoism adds a subversive element in viewing the world in a broader cosmos, made up of the five elements of gold, wood, water, fire, and earth, which includes animals and extra-ordinary creatures. More significantly it disdains the community-centred Confucian order in favour of individual freedom, which itself is a way of privileging nature (Dao) over culture (Confucianism).

Buddhism and Daoism in Chinese fiction are often of popular varieties that incorporate local and foreign (particularly Indian) myths and lore in such a way that the origins of its motifs, themes and tropes are not always traceable. Nevertheless, a pantheon of 'gods' headed by the Jade Emperor is discernible as the larger cosmological system that governs the Middle Kingdom based on combined Buddhist and Daoist principles. It is not surprising, then, that there is an abundance of stories about the worlds of the sea and sky and what lies beneath, above, between, and beyond, and their inhabitants, fairies, demons, and monsters.

The world of the sea, especially the dragon kingdoms that inhabit and control every lake, river, and sea, occupies a special place in Chinese mythology and fiction. Dragons are guardians of water, one of the five foundational elements of the cosmos, and play an important role in main-taining the health of the cosmos. They are responsible for generating and distributing cloud, rain, thunder, lightning, storm, flood, and drought. Dragon kingdoms are practically mirror images of kingdoms on the land (emperors on the land are spoken of as dragons). They have similar social and military hierarchies (including all sea creatures), albeit without the scholarly tier, and follow relatively similar code of conduct centered on the idea of loyalty. They too are answerable to the Jade Emperor.

Journey to the West

Dragons and humans, as equal members of the cosmos, interact regularly and their actions impact on each other's worlds. Disputes are not uncommon. In the 16th-century *Journey to the West* the dragons are instrumental in the story. The Monkey storms a dragon palace to acquire his weapon. Another dragon king files a 'wrongful death suit' against the Tang emperor Taizong with the king of the underworld. The dragon king is punished for disobeying a heavenly edict and causing 'unwritten' human suffering and death. The Tang emperor is dragged down to the underworld to answer to the charges and is, of course, exonerated at the end of the process. On his way back from the underground world he sees masses of spirits now suffering because they lived a corrupt life above ground. When he returns to his palace, he orders that true Buddhism be brought home from India, the West, and unleashes the journey to the West.

The novel, a fictional account of a real monk's travels to India to obtain Buddhist sutras, featuring his interactions with humans and non-humans, including dragons, is commonly

Figure 25. Tapestry with dragons and flowers, 11th to 12th century.

Figure 26. *The Classic of Filial Piety*, illustrated by Li Gonglin (Chinese, ca. 1041–1106), ca. 1085. Handscroll; ink and color on silk.

regarded as a satire of the Buddhist quest for enlightenment, the Daoist belief in magic, and the Confucian civil service system. The stories it contains are informed by ideologized views of the human condition, affirming, subverting, or rejecting the ways in which humans conduct themselves in the world. The novel is arguably about taming worldly desires – symbolized by the monk's flesh that is endlessly coveted by uncountable monsters and demons – as a first step towards enlightenment, *nirvana*, paving the way to individual salvation both here and in the Hereafter, premised on an enlightened life-style like the one prescribed in the *Nights*: to be good and to do good. When this set of ethics manifests itself in the person of an emperor, such as Tang Taizong, then the narrativized empire comes to resemble the ideal community of the *Nights*.

Paradoxically, as in the *Nights*, desire is often the mechanism through which subversion is staged. The satire of Confucianism, Buddhism, and Daoism here, it may also be argued, is found in the monk's lack of desire and, therefore, his lack of curiosity to distinguish between good and evil. He is more like al-Samandal in 'Jullanar', a '*mughaffal*' in Ibn al-Jawzi's words. He repeatedly falls into the traps of monsters and demons, always blind to their evil inten-tions and quick to admonish, punish or banish the Monkey, his one and only true champion, when the latter alerts him to the treachery ahead. Ambivalence towards desire, in pre-modern Chinese fiction, is in this sense very similar to that of the *Nights*, even though the details may seem on the surface quite different. This more-than-skin-deep similarity opens up a genuine vista for the two traditions to shed light on each other. 'The Story of Liu Yi' is a good example.

Liu Yi

'The Story of Liu Yi' by Li Chaowei belongs to the genre of *ch'uan-qi* fictional biography. It tells the story of a match made in heaven, so to speak, between an earthly scholar and a sea princess. It is a story of the interaction between the sea world and the land world very much in the vein of the *Nights* stories. Liu Yi is a young scholar on his way home, having failed in the civil service examination. He takes a detour to visit a friend and sees a strikingly beautiful but distressed woman on the roadside shepherding some sheep. He stops to offer help. She tells him that she is the youngest daughter of the dragon king of Lake Donting, married by her parents to the younger son of the dragon king of the River Jing. Her husband and parents-in-law have been mistreating her and, because she complained, she has been banished to the riverbank to shepherd the dragon rain workers. Would he, she begs, take a message to her parents to come for her rescue? He chivalrously agrees and before he take his leave, he asks, 'You will not avoid me once you get home, will you?', to which she replies, 'Of course not, I will treat you like family.'[6]

Liu Yi delivers the message to the king of Lake Donting and in a flash the dragon princess is rescued by her uncle, Lord Qiantang, and she is brought home with her full beauty and glory restored. In fact, before Liu Yi knows it, Lord Qiantang proposes that Liu Yi should marry her, and he turns down the proposal in anger only to regret his hasty refusal when he says goodbye to the princess. He returns home and becomes a rich man from the gifts given to him by the dragon kings. However, he is not a happy man. He moves from one place to another, and his wives keep dying on him. Finally, he marries for the third time a woman who reminds him of the dragon princess. When she bears him a son one year later, she reveals to him that she is indeed the dragon princess and that she has been in love with him since they first met. Through her he acquires immortality and together they live happily ever after.

'The Story of Liu Yi' may be read as a love story written very much in the *Nights* fashion. Its resemblance to 'Jullanar' is uncanny. Love, as we have seen in Chapter 3 on Jullanar's role as mother, is not the immediate gratification of desire but must endure the test of time. Liu Yi's initial stirring of attraction is immediately quashed by reason, in this case, defined by Confucian mores. Following the recognition scene, Liu explains to the dragon princess, now his wife, that his 'Freudian slip', referring to his earlier flirtation with her when he asked her to remember him, was not meant as an expression of feeling or love, even though later he thought only of her.

His initial rejection of her uncle's marriage proposal, a decision he immediately regretted, was in part a response to Lord Qiantang's crude and threatening way of making the offer. It was also required by his sense of honour and duty, since she had just separated from her dragon husband. The happiness he eventually earns, from the perspective of his moral universe, is premised on patience and endurance but, more importantly, on educating desire into love. The story tells us that even though he continuously thought of the dragon princess, he learns to love his third wife completely. He is lucky then that the wife whom he truly loves turns out to be the dragon princess whom he has not been able to forget. His sense of honour could have easily cost him his happiness if the dragon princess had been less persistent in pursuing her desire.

The dragon princess, recognizing his feelings, even as early as their first encounter, and his regret at refusing her uncle's offer, convinces her parents (who had almost married her to another dragon prince) to let her wait for him. When the right moment comes, she marries him as an ordinary land woman. She then patiently waits until she is certain of his love for her, more precisely after the birth of their son, and then discloses her identity. She clearly operates within a moral universe not hampered by the rules governing human behaviour. She may be careful, subtle, and emotionally intelligent in courting Liu Yi, but she also pursues her desire in a single-minded fashion. Her world allows her to do that without recrimination. She is like Jullanar, and her world resembles Jullanar's sea.

There is, however, a distinct difference: the world of the sea is not condemned as a hotbed of dark forces. On the contrary, it is a place where happiness can be found because, there, desire is not feared, barred or punished. Her uncle, Lord Qiantang, for example, is often guided by passion in his actions. At one time he was exiled after his impetuous behaviour caused several natural disasters. His rescue of his niece was equally impetuous. He takes immediate action as soon as he catches wind of his niece's distress. He practically wipes out the River Jing kingdom and the land communities around it. He does, like his niece, get results. His behaviour, rash from a certain perspective, is in this case rewarded despite all the killings that take place. His kingship is restored to him because his actions prove his worth as king – he has shown himself quick to right a wrong.

The juxtaposition of the land and sea in this Chinese story tells a tale of the role of desire in happiness. Liu Yi who follows the rules of his world is destined, it seems, to live an unfulfilled and unhappy life. He escapes only when his dragon princess rescues him from a fate worse than death and migrates to the sea. His happiness may be interpreted as his reward for righting a wrong, but it comes not from his world but another. Where desire is stifled, happiness is not possible. The contrast between his two lives is clear: disappointment and melancholy followed by prosperity and bliss. The system in place seems to stand in the way of happiness.

Liu Yi realizes this at the end. He forsakes this world completely and disappears into the sea, especially when the Tang emperor takes an interest in the supernatural and begins to recruit

people like Liu Yi to serve the empire. A relative, an official in the imperial system, has a
chance encounter with him years later, and
regards Liu Yi's freedom and happiness with
envy. 'You are destined to be an immortal and I
dried-up bones!' Liu Yi gives him fifty life-
prolonging pills and says, 'don't hang around in
the human world too long, you are just bringing
trouble onto yourself!'[7] Before long, his relative
disappears from this world too.

This story, it is clear, takes a jibe at the
Confucian way of life, particularly its domestication of desire. Liu Yi confesses that he was
stopped from expressing his feelings towards the
dragon princess by *li* (reason, equivalent to ʿ*aql*
in Arabic), and *yi* (loyalty the by-product of what
may be termed in Arabic as love). These two
defining principles of Confucianism are the
opposite poles of *qing*, which operates very much
like *hawa*; and *yu*, which is precisely *shahwa*.
The story exposes the potential for *li* and *yi* to
imprison Confucian scholars in a world of stagnation and unhappiness. More fundamentally, it
questions the Confucian worldview structured
by duty, premised on *li* and *yi* to the detriment of
happiness, and founded in part on the satisfac-
tion of *qing* and *yu*. In a brief epilogue, the author
Li Chaowei speaks tantalizingly of the intelligence, *lin*, of the non-human living creatures and
how, without the benefit of education, they
instinctually do the right things. He offers no
further explanation, but perhaps one may be
found in adjacent texts.

The period in which 'Liu Yi' was written, the ninth century, coincided with the proliferation of pseudo-historical writings on anomalies (extra-ordinary events, places and creatures) and of stories of the supernatural intruding on the human world (animals transmogrifying into humans and taking part in their life). These writings, scrutin-ized as 'strange writing' and 'the discourse on the foxes and ghosts', are said to be part of the dialo-gism taking place in Chinese culture before the tenth century, when Buddhism and Daoism were making inroads into Confucianism.

The supernatural, the strange, and the extra-ordinary help to create a world beyond that which is delineated by Confucianism. The cultural dialogue in 'Liu Yi' is between Daoism, which represents a form of multiculturalism in its absorption of 'local' popular traditions, and Confucianism, which is 'Han'-centric. This dialogue is often termed as a debate between nature and culture. 'Liu Yi' takes the side of nature, or Daoism, and exposes the limitation of the Confucian worldview and order. The sea, in this context, is the crux around which a chal-lenge to the land is constructed and whence this challenge is launched. Perhaps 'Abdallah the seaman's boycott of 'Abdallah the landman is similarly a challenge to the limitation of the worldview and order structuring the land.

Life beyond the Material World

Two stories in Arabic do what 'Liu Yu' does in Chinese. 'The City of Brass' invites contemplation on the ephemeral nature of human life on earth, while 'Hasib Karim al-Din' offers an alternative way of life. 'The City of Brass' is a rewriting of Solomon legends and as such it takes all the details from the *Tales of the Prophets* (*qisas al-anbiya*) and recasts the various discrete episodes into a story in which the different roles played by the various characters in each episode, such as the angels, demons, genies, ants, snakes, roc birds, horses, and monkeys, for example, are interlaced in such a way that a coherent world comes to life, or back to life, in the *Nights*.

City of Brass

The story is set in the Umayyad period and begins with the caliph ʿAbd al-Malik b. Marwan's wish to see a sample of the jars in which Solomon imprisoned the rebellious genies. He sends Musa b. Nasr (Nusayr), his governor in North Africa, to seek and fetch them. Accompanied by the vizier Talib b. Sahl and a wise old sheikh, ʿAbd al-Samad, Musa b. Nasr sets out and journeys through Solomon's kingdom, a vast dominion divided into parts, each ruled and inhabited by one of the angels or animals mentioned in the Qurʾan and the *Tales of the Prophets*, where only ruins of the magnificent cities and palaces Solomon had built are visible.

At one of these ruins, Musa encounters a demon locked in a column of black rock. This demon, called Dahish b. al-Aʿmash, smacks of Sakhr. The story he tells of how he ended up in the rock column is a variation of the Jarada story

Figure 27. Vintage illustration of 'The City of Brass' from *The Arabian Nights*, illustrated by Maxfield Parrish, 1909.

we encountered in Chapter 1. Dahish inhabits an idol and makes it come alive for an island kingdom of idol worshippers. The island's king has a most beautiful daughter who strikes Solomon's fancy. Solomon demands the king's submission to Islam and his daughter's hand.

The king refuses out of pride and at the instigation of Dahish. Solomon leads his gargantuan army to this island kingdom, devastates it, and imprisons Dahish in the rock column.

Much of 'The City of Brass' is like a cinematic recreation of Solomon legends in which these legends are retold only to assert the irretrievableness of the world they evoke. When Talib b. Sahl, upon arrival at the city of brass, tries to seize the treasures he sees, he is struck dead. There is a moral lesson for those who pay close attention, (*'ibra li-man i'tabara*), in all the stories of irrecoverable wonders from the past, such as Solomon's magical dominion, for the purpose of life is not power or riches but constant remembrance of God. Musa b. Nasr falls to his knees and weeps every time he hears a story of how death inevitably strikes human beings despite the splendour surrounding their life.

The poignancy of this message in 'The City of Brass' is accentuated by the mock historical context that frames it. Musa b. Nusayr is the commander who conquered North Africa on behalf of 'Abd al-Malik b. Marwan. The statement this story makes about conquest is obvious. Worse, 'Abd al-Malik is now seen as responsible for unleashing the demons onto humankind to wreak havoc in their world and life, as the other *Nights* stories reveal.

Hasib Karim al-Din

The story of 'Hasib Karim al-Din' escalates the existential anxiety palpable in 'The City of

Brass' and takes the moral lesson a step further. 'The City of Brass' ends with a quotation that 'God gave no one more than what he did Solomon, son of David'. What God gave him, which is still there for all to see, witness and experience, had not prevented Solomon's death. Similarly, 'Abd al-Malik's acquisition of some of Solomon's treasures did not prevent his death. As the story ends, 'Abd al-Malik is said to have handed over the Umayyad caliphate to his son and gone on a pilgrimage only to die on his way to Jerusalem. Death is the starting point of 'Hasib Karim al-Din' and its theme. It is not to be feared but welcomed as a site of contemplation.

In the *Nights*, the story of Hasib Karim al-Din, the son of a Greek sage, overlaps with those of two other youths, the Israelite prince Buluqiyya and the Afghani prince Jahanshah. Each leaves home for his own reasons and travels in Solomon's dominion, encountering fabulous living beings freed in the aftermath of Solomon's death. Woven together, their narratives tell one story of the search for wisdom cast in the form of two love stories framed by one of 'enlightenment'.

The frame story of 'Hasib Karim al-Din' begins with Daniel, a Greek sage, who loses his entire library except for five leaves. He bequeaths these to his unborn son and tells his wife:

Know that my death is near at hand and I am soon to leave this transitory world for the world of eternity. You are pregnant and it may be that you will give birth to a son after my

death. When you do, call him Hasib Karim
al-Din; give him the best of upbringings and
when he grows up and asks you what his
father left him by way of inheritance, give
him these five pages. When he reads them
and grasps their contents, he will become the
wisest person of his age.[8]

A son is of course born, but Hasib Karim al-Din
must journey through the entire cycle of stories
before he arrives at the point of asking for his
inheritance.

Growing up, Hasib Karim al-Din seems direc-
tionless and unable to earn a living. Eventually,
at his mother's insistence, he goes out with a
group of firewood collectors. When he finds jars
of honey in a well, the other firewood collectors
become greedy, take his share, and abandon him
there. He follows a scorpion and digs his way
out of the well into the cave of a serpent queen,
Yamlikha. She then tells him two stories, those
of Buluqiyya and Jahanshah, both as told to her
by Buluqiyya himself. As storyteller, she plays a
central role as the catalyst for Hasib Karim
al-Din's transformation from a hapless youth
into a wise vizier.

Buluqiyya
Buluqiyya finds out about Muhammad and the
future Muslim community from papers left
behind by his father and he leaves home in
search of Islam and its Prophet. He travels far
and wide, taking a tour of heaven and earth

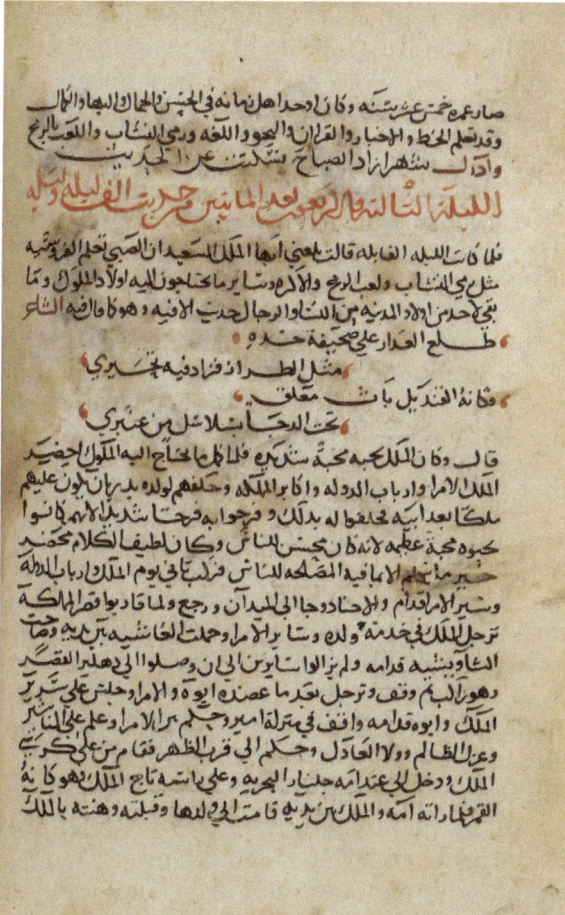

صار بعوجين عشرة سنة وكان واحدا هل بها به في الحسن الجمال والبها والكمال
وقرّطهم الخط والحساب والعلم والقرآن والنحو واللغة وبهي الأنساب والوقائع
وأدّب سهلان أذا أصبح بشكّست عن الكميرين

اللّيلة الثّالثة والأربعون بعد المايتين حديث القبلة وله

لمّا كان الّليلة القابلة قالت بلغني أنّها الملك المسعدان الأصبي لمّا العرق وبّه
مثل بالآداب والعلم والخط ولله ولد ووسايع ما حملوا وعليه اولاً للملوك وما
يفعل كذلك اهل المدينة من النساء والرجال لحبّ الابنه وهؤلاء هالفه الشعر

● طـلـع الـعـذار علـى صحيفـة خـدّه ●

● مثـل الـطّـرّاز فـراد فيه خـنجـري ●

● فكـأنّه الـقـنديل بـات معـلّـق ●

● تحـت الحـجـاب سـلاسل بـن عـنبـري ●

قال وكان ذلك الملك يحبّه سندبس فلمّا ظهر عليه ما احتاج اليه الملوك احضر
الملك لامر وارباب الدولة وكان بالملكه وحكّمهم لولده بدرابان بكون عليهم
ملكّا بعد ابيه حلفوا له بذلك ونجوا به وفرّحتا سنديل لامّه كانوا
بحبّه محبّة عظيمة لانّه رجيحسن لسانّ وكان لطيفا الكلام محمّد
خيرمّ جاه الامانيه المنصلحه لسانّ فذلّبا في يوم الملك واربابلدّوله
وسار الامّ اقدام والمحادث حا الى الجلّد آن رجع ولمّا قادوا وقادوا المكه
ترجل للملك في خدمته ولّن وسا راولّا ما وحلت الحاسنيه بنّ جّه وقّت
الدّعاوبنشيه قرامه ولم يزالوا ساوبس الى ان وصلوا الى هلدّا العشّر
دهورا لبيم ووقف وترحل بقّدرما عصّدرا ابوّه والامّا وحلّش على شهرّا
الملك وابوقلّامه واقف في بنزله سارود يحكّم مّا الاما وعلم عليّلناكّر
وعزّالظلّام ولا العّادل وحكّم الى قربّلّظهر فقا من عّلّا يكّ كريّ
الملك دخل لي عنّدامّه جّلّبارا بحرية وعلى باسّه تاج الملّك وهوّا كا نّه
القمّ غّارانّه امّه والملّك بن بّرّية قا مّتّالحّ للها وقّبلّبّه ونّه به بّالملّك

Figure 28. Page from the oldest known extant manuscript of the *Nights*.

and seeing with his own eyes the marvels that Solomon has left behind. He has many encounters with Solomon's former subjects, and even sees with his own eyes the dead Solomon with his magic ring still on his finger, lying still on a magnificent throne. On his journeys, Buluqiyya meets Jahanshah and Yamlikha.

The story of Jahanshah, a spoilt prince who goes out hunting with his father and gets lost at sea, is woven into the story of Buluqiyya. Buluqiyya encounters Jahanshah at two tombs that the latter built, one for his beloved wife, Shamsa, a genie princess, and the other for himself, for when he dies, so he can be buried next to Shamsa. This genie princess with whom Jahanshah falls in love, whose feathers he steals to keep her close, and for whom he abandons his father, is struck dead by a shark while taking a swim in a lake on one of their regular trips to her home kingdom. Buluqiyya's love for Muhammad parallels Jahanshah's passion for Shamsa. Both love stories end sadly. Buluqiyya never finds Muhammad, and Jahanshah loses his Shamsa to sudden death.

Buluqiyya's search for the elixir of immortality to keep him alive until he meets Muhammad leads him to Yamlikha. He finds instead a magic herb that will enable him and his evil companion, ʿAffan, to walk on water to Solomon's palace and treasures. Both quests, for immortality and for worldly riches and power, are futile. Buluqiyya never meets Muhammad, and ʿAffan's attempt to steal Solomon's ring ends disastrously.

'Affan, a man of great learning from Jerusalem, convinces Buluqiyya to drug Yamlikha in order to gain a magic herb, is burnt to a crisp by the fire bursting out of the serpent (not Yamlikha) protecting Solomon's dead body. Death takes all eventually, as the *Nights* insists, always ending a story with the inevitable 'arrival of the destroyer of all pleasures'. Only wondrous signs of God's might and grace will remain.

Back to Hasib Karim al-Din

Solomon's death ought to inspire contemplation and wisdom, not greed for material goods or hunger for power. In other words, the lesson in Solomon's death, that even the mightiest die, not from their mastery of the universe, which cannot be duplicated, as shown by the chaos brought by the afterlife of his dominion. Yamlikha's death in 'The story of Hasib Karim al-Din' is instrumental in imparting this lesson. She predicts her own death when she tells Hasib that if she lets him go home, he will betray her. She finally softens when even her subjects beg on his behalf. She makes him promise that he will never go to a bathhouse and lets him go. Hasib is tricked into a bathhouse by his king's clever vizier, Shamhur, who seeks her as only the broth made from her flesh will cure the king of all his ailments.

His life and world under threat, he reluctantly leads Shamhur to Yamlikha. The benevolent queen of serpents holds no grudge and instead comforts Hasib. She warns him that

Shamhur plots to murder the king and usurp power. She instructs Hasib to not drink the soup from the first batch as the vizier ordered him to do. He should rather drink the second, which the vizier intended to drink himself, and give the vizier the first, then give the king her flesh as well as some broth from the second batch. As it turns out, the first serving of soup is poisonous and the second medicinal. Shamhur dies a horrible death, whereas Hasib cures the king and is appointed the new vizier. More importantly, he is suddenly enlightened and now understands the five leaves of paper his sage father left behind. He too becomes the wisest man in his kingdom. It has taken Yamlikha's gruesome death to make him see light.

Death and Life Lessons

Death itself is not to be feared. It should be the catalyst for contemplative living centred on knowledge, awe and gratitude to God. The finality of life makes it especially urgent that human beings ought to live an exemplary life, as Hasib eventually does, serving his king and community wisely. However, human wisdom in the final analysis is minute in comparison with that of God. The five pages Hasib inherits from his father may be the epitome of human wisdom, but it pales by comparison to the immensity and incomprehensibility of the world Solomon has left behind.

Solomon's signet ring may not be a sign of his wisdom, but his wisdom is implied in how he ran his gargantuan and complex dominion. Having the ring helps, but ultimately it cannot answer all questions. The loss of the ring, eternal in the *Nights*, is only the beginning of long deliberations on the nature of power. Solomon's mastery of the universe was finite both temporarily and spatially. A prophet's wisdom, benevolence and might are minute next to God's. Buluqiyya's yearning for Muhammad and his journey in search of this beloved of God may at first sight seem the most devout things a Muslim could do, but in hindsight they are rather misguided. Ought not the real object of love be God Himself? After all, prophets are born and die but God is eternal and everlasting.

The world 'Hasib Karim al-Din' conjures is a pluriverse. In this pluriverse the present human world exists side by side with Solomon's kingdom and the non-human worlds he has left behind, such as the monkey kingdom, the sea world, and the world of demons and genies located on Mount Qaf. These worlds intrude on one another and, more importantly, generate together an expansive horizon of perspectives that allows us to see from afar the human world as only one of many. All these worlds participate in the politics of ideal community, particularly in the relationship between rule and justice; however, they diverge in the meaning of life. Hasib Karim al-Din returns to his community to serve as a vizier, but Jahanshah gives up his kingdom and devotes himself to guarding his wife's grave, while Buluqiyya continues his travels in search of Muhammad.

If the wonders of God's world never cease, the affairs of the community repeat themselves in a perpetual fashion, oscillating between good and evil, and justice and tyranny. Is Hasib Karim al-Din's choice to serve the king, then, better than the choices Jahanshah and Buluqiyya make? There is, it seems, more than one way of living and being, and each produces its own knowledge of the world, and know-how of living and being. Both types of knowledge are conditioned by lived experiences in 'this transitory world'.

According to Daniel, Hasib Karim al-Din's father, one can become 'the wisest person of his age' by mastering the five pages that have survived from his vast library. Compared with the wisdom of the prattling barber in 'The Hunchback', who is versed in all the sciences, Daniel and Hasib Karim al-Din's five pages seem more effective and useful. Perhaps this is beside the point. For, the pearls of wisdom hidden in those five pages become potent only after Hasib's adventures and his encounters with Buluqiyya and Jahanshah.

More important is the way 'Hasib Karim al-Din' tells us only about a transitory world here and now. The wondrous 'everlasting' pluriverse of which it is a small part remains beyond our grasp. Marouf in Mahfouz's rewriting of the *Nights* resembles Hasib, whose adventures in Solomon's world and experience with the magical ring, albeit only vicariously, prompt him to see beyond the fleeting wealth and power of this world. Similarly, Sindbad the Sailor returns, but only to live in yearning for the sea, for another world out there, and for a new unexpected journey.

Conclusion

'The sorting hat takes your choice into
account.'
'Really?'
'Really.'

J.K. Rowling (*Harry Potter and the
Deathly Hallows*)

In the 'Epilogue' to his seven adventures, Harry
Potter takes his children to King's Cross Station
to see his two sons off to Hogwarts. On Platform
9 ¾, where the Hogwarts Express is waiting for
the children to embark, he squats to tie the
shoelace of his younger son, Albus Severus
Potter, and at the same time assure him that he
will be a wonderful wizard whatever house he is
placed in, whether Slytherin (Voldemort's
house), or Gryffindor (Harry's and, as a student,
Dumbledore's house). His choice would matter,
for Harry Potter himself chose to be in Gryffindor.
While Slytherin broadly represents evil, and
Gryffindor good, good and evil are not set up in
a stark black-and-white binary. Professor Snape,
a Slytherin, was 'the bravest man' Harry Potter
has ever known. More importantly, no one is
born either good or evil. There is a Slytherin and

Figure 29. Platform nine and three quarters at London's King's Cross station.

Gryffindor in every living being, just as Voldemort and Dumbledore are integral parts of Harry Potter. Our greatest adventure is our journey of discovering what right and wrong are and of choosing to do right and to right wrongs.

Solomon legends and Harun al-Rashid myths in Arabic storytelling offer this journey of discovery in various forms. Concerning themselves with the human, these legends and myths scrutinize desire that drives our will to life as individual and social beings. Desire is paradoxical. It can lead to evil in the form of selfishness and antisocial behaviour. It can also lead to good, or love, which is in many ways the antithesis of desire. Love is loyalty to fellow human beings and the community and environment we all share. It consolidates our social relations and society. This loyalty can temper and tame our selfishness into sympathy with and care for others. It quite often manifests itself in 'taking no advantage', 'cheating no one', 'doing no harm', 'stealing nothing', and 'killing no life' in storytelling. Or, simply put, 'do not do to others what you do not wish upon yourself', as Confucius would say. For these seemingly simple acts are the foundation of communal harmony. They are informed by our sense that we are all equal. If these basic principles are violated, then it would be necessary to 'right the wrongs', which makes us feel that justice is served. Justice is the practical face of love.

Solomon legends and Harun al-Rashid myths, told as contests between passion and reason in the language of Arabic *adab* and storytelling, or between emotion and logic in our contemporary vocabulary, are fashioned from encounters between ideal community and real worlds. No two stories are the same because the encounter, as well as entanglement, between Barbieland and the real world, for example, take myriad forms. The real world is forever changing and at a very fast pace. The temptations the real world presents before us are shapeshifters, always stimulating new forms of desire that require comprehension anew and management differently. *Barbie* dramatizes the interplay between ideal community and the real world, and between the adventure in both, and the journey within effectively, and with a naughty sense of humour. As we take a good step towards ideal

Figure 30. 'The Storyteller', by James Bey. 1912.

community, we will come across further small wrong doings. For ideal community, in whichever form we imagine it, and precisely because it is imagined, always leaves out something important.

While Harun al-Rashid myths keep us firmly in our human world, Solomon legends remind us of the living beings who share our world. Human beings seem to have subordinated the other living beings to their rule and use, and exploited nature for their comfort and pleasure. They have reduced Solomon's pluriverse to our universe. Such a reminder is timely in several ways. Climate change and environmental crises draw our attention to our belligerent treatment of animals, insects, and plants, of nature, resources, and technology. The continuing and new conflicts around the world are exacerbating refugee and migration problems globally. Resources are dwindling and the radicalization of ideological positions is widespread. Social media, and even other forms of media, which on the surface offer a transnational space for dialogue and freedom of expression, are fanning the fire of radicalization, and cancel culture is spreading all around us. Othering is rearing an even uglier head than before. IT is fostering cyber gangsterism, inadvertently or otherwise, and generative AI is furthering cheating at schools.

We can no longer afford not to think of the world as 'a densely interconnected organic network', as James Bridle puts it in *Ways of*

Being: Animals, Plants, Machines, The Search for a Planetary Intelligence (2023). This network of humans, animals, plants, and machines requires a language that allows us to 'speak about and through and with the world'. For example, what do we do with AI? Do we use it to cheat or help us with honest excellence? How? Arabic *adab* and Chinese *wen* offer a blueprint for engagement with and comprehension of the emerging changes in the material conditions of our living summarized in a simple motto: 'do not do to others what you do not wish upon yourself'. Understanding the potential good and evil of these new conditions, and the benefit and harm they can generate for ourselves and others, we will be able to find a language to help us negotiate the new challenges, articulate our vision for communal harmony, and refine our ethics of living for today. *Adab*, *wen*, and the humanities in general show us that it is possible, and necessary, to strike a balance between doing what's right and enjoying a good life.

Glossary

adab Literature, or literary arts, or literary culture.

adib A man of letters, men educated in the literary arts, a cultured man.

addad sg. *did* Used in plural only when it denotes a category of words that contain a meaning and its opposite at the same time.

'adl Justice; used synonymously with *insaf*, means equal treatment of all people.

akhbar sg. *khabar* Anecdotes, also a genre of history that comprises anecdotes.

Alf layla wa layla The *Thousand and One Nights* is the name given to a body of stories in Arabic that come from divergent sources and exist in diverse texts.

'aql Reason; juxtaposed to passion, *hawa,* it denotes the ability to control emotions and make decisions that will not result in harm of the individual or community.

'aqil pl. *'aqilun* Reasonable people, people who possess reason.

'ayyar pl. *'ayyarun* Vagabonds; originally a class of soldier or a mercenary who kept neighbourhoods safe during Abbasid times.

fitna Distraction; it refers to physical attributes, such as beauty in looks or

	voice, or actions that distract a person from reasonable behaviour and proper conduct.
framing, frame-tale, enframed story	Framing is a storytelling technique in the *Thousand and One Nights.* Like Russian dolls, one story embeds another story and yet other stories in such a way that each story is a cycle of stories. The frame-tale begins and ends the cycle, with the enframed stories.
futuwwa	Young strong men; derived from *fata*, a term used in early Arabic writings to describe 'Ali ibn Abi Talib, the Prophet's young and eloquent cousin and son-in-law, and the last of the Four Rightly Guided Caliphs.
hammam	Public bath house; many events in stories of The *Thousand and One Nights* occur in the hammam.
hawa	Passion; juxtaposed to reason, *'aql*, it describes the extremity of an emotion, which can be love or hate, anger or jealousy, that leads to madness or actions that result in chaos.
hikayat sg. *hikaya*	tales, as in *Hikayat alf layla wa layla* tales of one thousand and one nights
hikma	Wisdom; it describes the quality of a story, a person or a knowledge tradition.
hubb or *mahabba*	love.
humq or *hamaqa*	Foolishness.

'ibra li-man i'tabara	A lesson for one who will learn from it.
'iffa	Uprightness.
ikhwan sg. *akh*	Brother or brothers.
'ilm	Knowledge or science, coeval with *iman* of faith in Arabic-Islamic writings.
iman	Faith.
'ishq	Excessive desire and love that lead to passion.
jawari sg. *jariya*	Slave-girl or slave-girls.
jaza'	Anguish; the opposite of patience, *sabr* (below), it can lead to debilitating sadness or even madness.
lusus sg. *liss*	Thief.
al-madina al-fadila	Virtuous city, al-Farabi's term for the ideal community or utopia.
al-madina al-fasiqa	Sinful city, al-Farabi's term for dystopia.
mirrors for princes	Epitomized by *Kalila wa Dimna*, it refers to a genre of works intended to provide instructions for the sovereign and his officers on the protocols of just rule in a kingdom.
muhtal	Trickster, con artist; the protagonist of many stories in *Adab* and the *Thousand and One Nights*.
qisas	Stories.
qisas al-anbiya'	Stories or lives of the prophets; the stories are found in historical narratives and exegesis of the Qur'an, and they also constitute an independent genre of storytelling in Arabic.
sabr	The opposite of anguish, *jaza'*; patience, endurance.
sawt	Tune or melody.

shahwa	Desire; quite often of the unhealthy type that leads to excess.
shatir sg. *shuttar*	Larrikins or strong men; they are the protagonists and supporting characters of many stories in the *Thousand and One Nights*.
sira sha'biyya	Popular epics; it refers to a genre of storytelling written in the middle register of the Arabic language. These epics are historical in the main, but one revolves around a con artist, 'Ali al-Zaybaq.
sadaqa	Friendship; it denotes loyalty among men and women.
suhba	Companionship; the foundation of friendship and used interchangeably with *sadaqa*.
tarikh	History.
ulfa	Familiarity, intimacy resulting from people living in proximity with each other.
qing	Desire, emotion, passion; it also denotes unbreakable emotional ties as well as another form of intelligence in Chinese.
haohan	Good men, heroes; close to *fata* and *shatir* in Arabic.
kung fu	Martial arts; as a term it is known through the Hong Kong film genre made famous and popular by Bruce Lee.
li	Reason; very close to the Arabic 'aql, it denotes the human being's critical faculty as well as its training.
lin	Intelligence.
muyi tianxia	A phrase describing the role of the empress as the mother of all that lie under the heaven.

wen	Literature, literary arts, literary culture.
wenren	Men of letters, men educated in the literary arts, cultured men.
wulun	The five social relationships in Confucianism.
wuxia	Martial artist, knight-errant; a genre of Chinese storytelling, in literature or film, centred around itinerant martial artists who right wrongs and maintain justice outside the state structure, a way of life, and a vision of the world in which men and women can live meaningfully without joining the state bureaucracy.
xiake	Itinerant martial artists, knight-errants; they are the protagonists of a large body of Chinese storytelling.
xiao	Filial duty to parents.
yi	Loyalty to friends.
yu	Desire for love, wealth and power.
zhong	Loyalty to sovereign and country.

Notes

Introduction

1 Stefan Sperl, 'Man's "Hollow Core": Ethics and Aesthetics in Hadith Literature and Classical Arabic Adab.' *Bulletin of the School of Oriental and African Studies, University of London* 70, no. 3 (2007), pp. 459–86.

Chapter 1. Virtuous City: Sovereign, Courtier, Subject

1 Husain Haddawy, trans., *The Arabian Nights* (New York, 1990), pp. 31–32.
2 Haddawy, *Arabian Nights*, p. 48.
3 Haddawy, *Arabian Nights*, p. 47.
4 Haddawy, *Arabian Nights*, p. 35.
5 Haddawy, *Arabian Nights*, p. 45.
6 Ibn al-Jawzi discusses in detail the role of reason in controlling desire and passion variously in *Dhamm al-hawa*, ed. Mustafa 'Abd al-Wahid, rev. Muhammad al-Ghazali (Cairo, 1962); idem, *Akhbar al-hamqa wa'l-mughaffalin* (Beirut, 1988); and idem, *Kitab al-adhkiya'* (Beirut, 1966).
7 Ibn al-Muqaffa', *Kalila wa Dimna*, ed. Salim Shams al-Din (Beirut, 2002).
8 al-Farabi, *Mabadi ara' ahl al-madina al-fadila*, trans., Richard Walzer as *On the Perfect State* (Oxford, 1985), p. 249.
9 For a fuller account and detailed analysis of 'The Merchant and the Genie' and 'The Fisherman and the Demon' in relation to other stories in the

Nights, see Wen-chin Ouyang, 'Utopian Fantasy or Dystopian Nightmare: Trajectories of Desire in Classical Arabic and Chinese Fiction', in *Le repertoire narrative arabe medieval: transmission et ouverture,* ed. Aboubakr Chraibi, Frederic Bauden and Antonella Ghersetti (Geneva: Droz, 2008), pp. 323–351.

10 For a detailed analysis, see Wen-chin Ouyang, 'Solomon's Ring', in *The Qur'an and Adab: the Shaping of Literary Traditions in Classical Islam,* ed. Nuha Al-Shaar (Oxford, 2007), pp. 433–471.

11 Ahmad b. Muhammad al-Thaʿlabi, *Qisas al-anbiyaʾ al-musamma ʿAraʾis al-majalis* (Beirut, n.d.), trans., William A. Brinner as *Lives of the Prophets* (Leiden, Boston, Koln, 2002), p. 539.

12 Brinner, *Lives of the Prophets*, p. 540.

Chapter 2. Heroic Family: Love, Desire, Marriage

1 André Clot, *Harun al-Rashid and the World of the Thousand and One Nights*, trans., John Howe (London, 1986); Milton Klonsky, *The Fabulous Ego; Absolute Power in History* (New York, 1974).

2 Aḥmad Amin, *Harun al-Rashid* (London, 2014). Available at: https://www.hindawi.org/books/51719608/ last accessed 31 August 2021; Muhammad 'Abd al-Rahman Yunus. *al-Istibdad al-sultawi wa'l-fasad al-jinsi fi alf layla wa layla* (Beirut, 2007).

3 For example, Shawqi Abu Khalil, *Harun al-Rashid: amir al-kulafaʾ wa ajall muluk al-dunya* (Beirut, 1996); Aḥmad al-Qattan and Muhammad Tahir al-Zayn in *Harun al-Rashid: al-khalifa al-mazlum* (Alexandria, 2001); Hasan ʿAbd al-Ghaffar in *Harun al-Rashid: al-khalifa al-muftara ʿalayhi* (Giza, 2009).

4 Haddawy, *Arabian Nights*, p. 151.

5 Haddawy, *Arabian Nights*, p. 151.
6 Haddawy, *Arabian Nights*, p. 151.
7 Haddawy, *Arabian Nights*, p. 206.
8 The *Nights* and the *Tales of the Marvellous* both refer to Muhammad b. Sulayman al-Zaynabi, the historical governor of Basra, as 'king'.
9 For a fuller plot account and analysis of these stories, see Wen-chin Ouyang, 'Harun al-Rashid in Premodern Arabic Literary Imaginary: Ideology of Monogamy, Harem Politics, and Court Intrigues', in *The Historian of Islam at Work: Essays in Honor of Hugh N. Kennedy*, ed. Maaike van Berkel and Letizia Osti (Leiden, 2022), pp. 340–355.
10 Andras Hamori, 'Notes on Two Love Stories from the *Thousand and One Nights*', *Studia Islamica* 43 (1975), pp. 65–80.
11 For a fuller plot outline and discussion of this *sira*, see Wen-chin Ouyang, 'Romancing the Epic: 'Umar al-Nu'man as narrative of empowerment', *Arabic and Middle Eastern Literatures*, 3: 1 (2000), pp. 5–18, and 'The Epical Turn of Romance: Love in the Narrative of 'Umar al-Nu'man', *Oriente Moderno*, 19: 1 (2002), pp. 485–504.
12 See David Quint, *Epic and Empire* (Princeton, 1993).
13 Malcolm C. Lyons, trans., *The Arabian Nights: Tales of 1001 Nights*, 3 vols. (London, 2008), vol. 1, p. 509.
14 Ibn Hazm, *Tawq al-hamama*, ed. Salah al-Din al-Qasimi (Tunis, n.d.)

Chapter 3. Harmonious Community: Fathers and Mothers, Sons and Daughters

1 Malcolm C. Lyons, trans., *Tales of the Marvellous and News of the Strange* (London, 2014), pp. 333–4.
2 Lyons, *Tales of the Marvellous*, p. 350.

3   Lyons, *Tales of the Marvellous*, p. 355.
4   For a detailed analysis, see Ouyang, 'Utopian Fantasy or Dystopian Nightmare', pp. 323–351.
5   J. R. Rowling, *Harry Potter and the Order of the Phoenix* (London, 2003).
6   Haddawy, *Arabian Nights*, p. 383.
7   Haddawy, *Arabian Nights*, p. 399.

Chapter 4. Alternative Society: The Fellowship of Men and Women

1   Haddawy, *Arabian Nights*, p. 189.
2   Haddawy, *Arabian Nights*, p. 206.
3   Abu Hayyan al-Tawhidi, *al-Sadaqa wa'l-sadiq*, ed. 'Ali Mutawalli Salah (Cairo, 1972), p. 2.
4   Tawhidi, *al-Sadaqa wa'l-sadiq*, pp. 1–2.
5   Nuha Alshaar, *Ethics in Islam: Friendship in the Political Thought of al-Tawhidi and his Contemporaries* (London, 2014).
6   Martin Huang, *Male Friendship in Ming China* (Leiden, 2006).
7   Al-Tawhidi, *al-Sadaqa wa'l-sadiq*, p. 2.
8   For a fuller account and analysis of these stories, see Ouyang, 'An Ethical Underworld?: Legendary Con Artists in Arabic Vernacular Fiction', *Oriente Moderno*, LXXXIX (2009), pp. 407–424.
9   Al-Tawhidi, *al-Sadaqa wa'l-sadiq*, p. 2.
10   For a detailed analysis, see Wen-chin Ouyang, 'صداقة الرجال والأخوّة في الثقافتين العربية والصينية / Male Friendship and Brotherhood in Arabic and Chinese Cultures,' *Alif: Journal of Comparative Poetics*, 36 (2015), pp. 145–172.

Chapter 5. *Joie de Vivre*: Life is a Banquet

1   Ulrich Marzolph (email dated 14 June 2017).
2   Haddawy, *The Arabian Nights*, pp. 206–207.
3   Haddawy, *Arabian Nights*, p. 295.

4 Haddawy, *Arabian Nights*, p 173.

5 Haddawy, *The Arabian Nights*, p. 157.

6 Haddawy, *The Arabian Nights*, p. 157.

7 Haddawy, *Arabian Nights*, p. 162.

8 Haddawy, *The Arabian Nights*, pp. 169–70.

9 Haddawy, *The Arabian Nights*, p. 170

10 Haddawy, *The Arabian Nights,* p. 185.

11 Haddawy, *The Arabian Nights*, pp. 172–3.

12 Haddawy, *Arabian Nights*, p. 161.

13 Haddawy, *Arabian Nights*, p. 190.

14 Haddawy, *Arabian Nights*, p. 195.

15 Haddawy, *Arabian Nights*, p. 185.

16 Haddawy, *Arabian Nights*, p. 189.

17 Haddawy, *Arabian Nights*, p. 185.

18 Haddawy, *Arabian Nights*, p. 185.

19 Haddawy, *Arabian Nights*, p. 164.

20 Haddawy, *Arabian Nights*, p. 185.

21 Haddawy, *Arabian Nights*, p. 188.

22 For detailed analysis, see Wen-chin Ouyang, 'Trickster Jester: on humour, word play and laughter in the Arabian Nights', in *Festschrift zum 65. Geburtstag von Ulrich Marzolph Vol. 1,* ed. Regina Bendix and Dorothy Noyes (Dortmund: Verlag für Orientkunde, 2018), pp. 32–58; and 'Coincidence and Entanglement: Wonder and Framing in *The Thousand and One Nights*', *Journal of Arabic and Islamic Studies*, 24: 1 (2024), pp. 189–208.

Chapter 6. Heaven on Earth: Storytelling and Meanings of Life

1 Naguib Mahfouz. *Layali alf layla* (Cairo, 1989), trans. Denys Johnson-Davis as *Arabian Nights and Days* (New York, 1995).

2 For a detailed analysis of Mahfouz's novel in relation to the *Nights* and the imagining of a modern

nation, see Wen-chin Ouyang, *Poetics of Love in The Arabic Novel: Nation-State, Modernity and Tradition* (Edinburgh: Edinburgh University Press, 2012).

3 Mahfouz, *Arabian Nights and Days*, p. 216.

4 Mahfouz, *Arabian Nights and Days*, pp. 211–15.

5 For a fuller account, see Ouyang, 'Utopian Fantasy or Dystopian Nightmare', pp. 323–351.

6 *Taiping guangji*, vol. 9, p. 3411. Translated into English and adapted by David Hawkes as *Liu Yi and the Dragon Princess: A Thirteenth Century Zaju Play by Shang Zhong-xian* (Hong Kong, 2003); translations in this volume are my own.

7 *Taiping guangji*, vol. 9, p. 3417.

8 Lyons, *Arabian Nights,* vol. 2, p. 363.

Further Reading and Viewing

The *Thousand and One Nights*, widely popular among scholars and students of Arabic and world literature, continues to generate critical reflection and discussion. Books, articles, and book chapters abound on the manuscripts and texts of *Alf layla wa-layla*, translations, adaptations in films and novels, individual stories, storytelling techniques, and motifs and themes. An up-to-date bibliography compiled by Ulrich Marzolph is available online (https://wwwuser. gwdguser.de/~umarzol/arabiannights-i.html). *The Arabian Nights Encyclopedia* he co-edited with Richard van Leeuwen in 2004, also available online (https://www.arvindguptatoys.com/ arvindgupta/Arabian%20Nights.pdf), offers a comprehensive list and summaries of the stories. Robert Irwin's *The Arabian Nights: A Companion* (London: Allen Lane, 1994), remains the most comprehensive and accessible introduction. Marina Warner's *Stranger Magic: Charmed States & the Arabian Nights* (London: Chatto & Windus, 2011) offers a nuanced critical assessment of the influence of *The Arabian Nights* in Europe. Ferial J. Ghazoul's *Nocturnal Poetics: The Arabian Nights in Comparative Context* (Cairo: American University in Cairo Press, 1996) brings the Arabic and European perspectives together. For readers of Arabic

and/or French, a must is Abdelfattah Kilito's
*L'oeil et l'aiguille: Essais sur "Les Mille et une
nuits"* (Paris: La Découverte, 1992), Arabic
translation by Mustafa al-Nahhal as *al-'Ayn wa'l
ibra: dirasa fi "alf layla wa-layla"* (Casablanca:
al-Fank, 1996).

Kalila wa-Dimna, the epitome of the 'mirror
for princes' genre of storytelling and writing,
has always been integral to research on *adab* but
has only recently generated a large-scale interest
in its multilingual origins, diverse manuscript
traditions, and impact on world literature.
Information on the ten-year project led by
Beatrice Gruendler is available online (https://
www.geschkult.fu-berlin.de/en/e/kalila-wa-
dimna/index.html).

Qisas al-anbiya', a body of stories central to
religious studies, historiography and storytelling,
has similarly been central to the study of
Muslim civilization, but has yet to generate
literary interest. Marianna Klar's *Interpreting
al-Tha'labi's Tales of the Prophets: Temptation,
Responsibility and Loss* (Abingdon: Routledge,
2009) is an important contribution.

Al-Sira al-sha'biyya, the popular epic in
Arabic, is another genre of storytelling that has
yet to attract wider attention and recognition.
Beside Malcolm Lyon's three-volume study, *The
Arabian Epic* (Cambridge: Cambridge University
Press, 1995), which introduces the readers to the
main epics and offers synopses, there have only
been two books on two of the epics: Peter Heath's

The Thirsty Sword: Sirat 'Antar and the Arabic Popular Epic. (Leiden: Brill, 1996), and Helen Blatherwick's. *Prophets, Gods and Kings in Sirat Sayf Ibn Dhi Yazan: An Intertextual Reading of an Egyptian Popular Epic* (Leiden: Brill, 2016).

Adab has similarly been central in discussions of premodern Arabic literature, but given its diversity, scholarship on this broad area of Arabic writings tends to focus on specific topics. Andras Hamori looks at the craft of poetry and story in *On the Art of Medieval Arabic Literature* (Princeton, NJ: Princeton University Press, 1974); *Writing and Representation in Medieval Islam: Muslim Horizons*, ed. Julia Bray (Routledge Studies in Middle Eastern Literatures. London: Routledge, 2006), homes in on representation; while James Montgomery contemplates Islamic cosmology in *Al-Jahiz: In Praise of Books* (Edinburgh: Edinburgh University Press 2013). Philip Kennedy's *Recognition in the Arabic Narrative Tradition: Discovery, Delivery and Delusion* (Edinburgh: Edinburgh University Press, 2016) is one of the rare works that offer comparative reflections on The *Thousand and One Nights*, *Tales of the Prophets*, and the *Maqamat* stories of a con artist through the lens of a narrative technique, 'recognition'. Two books by Abdelfattah Kilito are delightfully illuminating: *L'Auteur et ses doubles: Essai sur la culture arabe classique* (Paris: Seuil, 1985), Arabic translation by 'Abd al-Salam Bin 'Abd al-'Ali, *al-Kitaba wa'l-tanasukh: Mafhum al-mu'allif fi'l-thaqafa al-ʿArabiyya* (Beirut: Dār al-Tanwīr, 1985), English translation by Michael Cooperson, *The Author and His Doubles* (Syracuse: Syracuse University Press, 2001); and *Les Arabes et l'art du récit: une étrange familiarité* (Paris: Actes Sud, 2009), English translation by Mbarek Sryfi, *Arabs and the Art of Storytelling: A Strange Familiarity* (Syracuse: Syracuse University Press, 2014).

The Classic Chinese Novel is of course one of the most important topics of research in classical Chinese literature. Margaret Berry's *The Chinese Classic Novels: An Annotated Bibliography of Chiefly English-Language Studies* (London: Routledge, 2010) is a useful resource. The following are classics in the field: Wilt L. Idema, *Chinese Vernacular Fiction: The Formative Period* (Leiden: Brill, 1979); Chih Tsing Hsia, *The Classic Chinese Novel: A Critical Introduction* (Bloomington: Indiana University Press, 1980); Patrick Hanan, *The Chinese Vernacular Story* (Cambridge MA: Harvard University Press, 1981); Hegel, Robert E. Hegel, *The Novel in Seventeenth-Century China* (New York: Columbia University Press, 1981); Andrew H. Plaks, *The Four Masterworks of the Ming Novel* (Princeton: Princeton University Press, 1987); and Liangyan Ge, *Out of the Margins: The Rise of the Chinese Vernacular Fiction* (Honolulu: University of Hawai'i Press, 2001).

For those who wish to get a sense of the world of chivalry in premodern Chinese stories, they might find it fun to turn to films and television dramas adapted from or modelled on them:

Films

Detective Dee and the Mystery of the Phantom Flame. 2010. Dir. Tsui Hark.

Young Detective Dee: Rise of the Sea Dragon. 2013. Dir. Tsui Hark.

Detective Dee: The Four Heavenly Kings. 2018. Dir. Tsui Hark.

Red Cliff I. 2008. Dir. John Woo.

Red Cliff II. 2009. Dir. John Woo.

Red Cliff (abridged version). 2009. Dir. John Woo.

Television Drama

Langya Bang (Nirvana in Fire I; 54 episodes). 2015. Dir. Kong Sheng and Li Xue. Available on YouTube with English subtitles.

Langya Bang: Fengqi Changlin (Nirvana in Fire II; 50 episodes). 2017. Dir. Kong Sheng and Li Xue. Available on YouTube with English Subtitles.

Sanguo (Three Kingdoms; 95 episodes). 2010. Dir. Gao Xixi. Available on YouTube with English subtitles.

Sanguo Yanyi (Romance of the Three Kingdoms; 84 episodes). 1994. Dir. Wu Xiaodong. Available on YouTube.

On the public value of global humanities, Italo Calvino in *Why Read the Classics*, tr. Martin McLaughlin (London: Penguin, 1999), Helen H. Small in *The Value of the Humanities* (Oxford: Oxford University Press, 2016), and Jonathan Bate in *The Public Value of the Humanities* (London: Bloomsbury Academic, 2011) make arguments on which one might base a compelling case for the immediate relevance of *adab*, *wen* and literature today. David Abram in *The Spell of the Sensuous: Perception and Language in a More-Than-Human World* (New York: Vintage Books, 1996) and *Becoming Animal: An Earthly Cosmology* (New York: Random House, 2010), and James Bridle in *Ways of Being: Animals, Plants, Machines: The Search for a Planetary Intelligence* (London: Penguin, 2023) extend the scope of the humanities to include animals and machines.

List of Illustrations

Figure 1. 19th-century Urdu translation of the *Thousand and One Nights*. 2
Munshī 'Abdulkarim, translator. 'Alf lailah Urdū'. [Kanpur, India:] Matba' Muṣṭafā'ī, 1263 [1847]. South Asian Rare Book Collection, Library of Congress Asian Division.

Figure 2. A storyteller reciting from the *Arabian Nights* in Cairo. 7
J.B. Lippincott Company: Philadelphia and Hurst & Blackett, Ltd.: London, 1911. p 28. Image used under a CC BY-SA 2.5 licence.

Figure 3. Book of Daniel and Solomon's Proverbs. 11
Arabic Manuscripts 597. Library of Congress Collection of Manuscripts in St. Catherine's Monastery, Mt. Sinai.

Figure 4. Talismanic scroll bearing 'Solomon's seal'. 22
Metropolitan Museum of Art, New York. Gift of Nelly, Violet and Elie Abemayor, in memory of Michel Abemayor, 1978.

Figure 5. Seal ring. 23
Metropolitan Museum of Art, New York. Rogers Fund, 1912.

Figure 6. 'The Story of the Fisherman'. 26
Image used under a CC0 1.0 licence.

Figure 7. 'Genie of the Lamp'. 35
AF Fotografie / Alamy Stock Photo E1B48E.

Figure 8. Mirror showing Solomon. 39
Metropolitan Museum of Art, New York. Gift
of Florence E. and Horace L. Mayer, 1978.

Figure 9. 'The Fisherman and the Genie'. 42
Chronicle / Alamy Stock Photo 2XMYA83.

Figure 10. 'The Fisherman and the Afrite
(or Genie)'. 47
Metropolitan Museum of Art, Drawings and
Prints, Harris Brisbane Dick Fund, 1936
36.27.1(2).

Figure 11. 'Haroun al-Raschid'. 54
Project Gutenburg, eBook #12788.

Figure 12. **56**
Kremlin Pool / Alamy Stock Photo F4H9HA.

Figure 13. 'Majnun in the wilderness'. 58
AKM282.36 © The Aga Khan Museum.

Figure 14. Manuscripts of *Mi'a layla wa layla*
and *Kitab al-Jaghrafiya*. 65
AKM513. © The Aga Khan Museum.

Figure 15. Still from *The Fellowship of the Ring*
(dir. Peter Jackson, 2001). 79
Moviestore Collection Ltd / Alamy Stock
Photo BKDHE3.

Figure 16. Scene from *The Adventures of
Prince Achmed* (dir. Lotte Reiniger, 1926). 82
Sueddeutsche Zeitung Photo / Alamy Stock
Photo TA2D7T.

Figure 17. Manuscript folio of *Yusuf and
Zulaykha*. 87
AKM229. © The Aga Khan Museum

Figure 18. Chinese stamp.   106
Zhang Jiahan / Alamy Stock Photo RN5TDY.

Figure 19. Illustration from *The Three
Kingdoms*.   107
Library of Congress, Asian Division, Chinese
Rare Books.

Figure 20. *Water Margin* block-print.   111
OA 102-145(MS).

Figure 21. Still from Sindbad (dir. Karel
Zeman, 1974).   126
Photo 12 / Alamy Stock Photo B7YEG3.

Figure 22. Illustration for 'Sindbad the Sailor'. 127
Private collection/Bridgeman Images.

Figure 23. Still from *Barbie* (dir. Greta Gerwig,
2023).   129
Imago / Alamy Stock Photo 2WY0KDA.

Figure 24. 'The Wedding Banquet'.   142
CPA Media Pte Ltd / Alamy Stock Photo
2B01FY4.

Figure 25. Tapestry with dragons and
flowers.   157
Metropolitan Museum of Art, New York.
Fletcher Fund, 1987.

Figure 26. Illustration by Li Gonglin from
The Classic of Filial Piety.   158
Metropolitan Museum of Art, New York.
Ex coll.: C. C. Wang Family, From the P. Y. and
Kinmay W. Tang Family Collection, Gift of
Oscar L. Tang Family, 1996.

Figure 27. Illustration by Maxfield Parrish
from 'The City of Brass', in *The Arabian Nights:
Their Best-Known Tales*, ed. K. D. S. Wiggin et al.

(New York: Charles Scribner's Sons, 1909). PDF, image 267. https://www.loc.gov/item/09028132/.167 Library of Congress, 09028132.

Figure 28. Manuscript folio of the *Nights*.   171
Bibliothèque nationale de France.
Département des Manuscrits. Arabe
3609-3611.

Figure 29. Photograph of platform nine and
three quarters.   179
Cristian Storto / Alamy Stock Photo PCYT8H.

Figure 30. 'The Storyteller', by James Bey.   181
Tangier American Legation Institute for
Moroccan Studies.

Index

''Abdallah the Landman
    and 'Abdallah the
    Seaman', 151–3
adab
    Badr al-Din and, 139
    definition of, 6–7
    education in, 144
    ethics of living, and, 8,
        183
    hadith, and, 6
    Harun al-Rashid, and,
        12, 53, 56, 59,
        181
    joie de vivre, and, 124,
        128, 183
    justice (*'adl*), and,
        39–40
    love and loyalty in, 24
    reason (*'aql*), and,
        39–40, 94, 103, 122
    relevance to modern
        world, 7
    satire of, 134–8
    Solomon stories, and,
        12, 181
    *Thousand and One
        Nights*, and, 57,
        67
    'The Two Viziers', and,
        144

wen, and, 4–7, 8
wulun, and, 15
Ahmad Amin, 52
Ahmad al-Danif, 113, 114,
    118, 119
'Aladdin with Moles on
    His Cheeks',
    115–16, 120
''Ali b. Bakkar and Shams
    al-Nahar', 59, 64–5
''Ali Shar and Zumurrud',
    115
'Ali al-Zaybaq, 114, 118
al-Amin, 62, 63, 86
'Anis al-Jalis and Nur
    al-Din b. Khaqan'
    65–8
Arabic literature
    'adl, 34, 40
    'aql, 38–41, 44–8, 164
    brotherhood, 100
    code of conduct, 9–10,
        13, 48–51
    crisis in the
        humanities, and, 8
    definition of, 4–5
    epic stories, 5, 18, 112,
        113–16, 124
    ethical purpose of, 8–9
    father figures, 80–91

friendship, 102–4,
    105–6, 112
hawa, 42–8
heroes, 80
hikma, 40
historical commentary/
    tradition as to, 154
humq, 41
'iffa, 40
joie de vivre, 128
justice, 118, 120, 121,
    122–3
law, 116–17
love, 72, 120, 121,
    122–3, 164
love stories, 56
mother figures, 81,
    91–8
outlaws, 116–17
passion, 120, 121,
    122–3
relationships, 24
search for paradise,
    15
self-discovery, 125
sisterhood, 100
storytelling, 12, 100,
    122, 125, 126, 128,
    151, 180–1
tradition of reading of,
    5
writing, 12
See also Harun
    al-Rashid; Solomon,
    King; *Thousand and
    One Nights*

artificial intelligence, 183
'Aziz and 'Aziza, 71
    See 'Umar al-Nu'man'

Barbie (dir. Greta Gerwig,
    2023), 128–9, 146,
    181
beauty, 128–9, 130, 135,
    137, 138, 139, 141,
    146, 150
behaviour, 109, 129, 130,
    138, 162, 163, 180
Buddhism, 14, 15, 154,
    155, 156, 159, 165
Buluqiyya, 169, 170–3,
    175–6

Cao Cao, 82, 108, 119
children *See* family
Chinese dynasties
    Han Dynasty, 83, 108
    Jin Dynasty, 108
    Song Dynasty, 120
    Spring and Autumn
        Period, 104
    Tang Dynasty, 1, 83
    Warring States Period,
        105
    Yuan Dynasty, 106
    Zhou Dynasty, 104
Chinese literature
    brotherhood, 19
    cinema adaptations,
        198
    code of conduct, 9–10,
        13

desire, 153, 159
ethical purpose of, 8–9
father figures, 18, 19, 56, 80–4
fiction stories, 153–5
freedom, 15
friendship, 104–13
haohan, 116, 117–18
historical tradition of, 154
justice, 120–3
kung fu films and, 116
law, 116–17
love, 120–3, 153
mother figures, 18, 19, 56, 80–4
mythologising of rulers, 81–2
mythology within, 155
otherworld, 165–77
outlaws, 116–17
passion, 120–3
pseudo-historical writings, 165
religion and, 14
romances, 4
sea, 155, 163
search for paradise, 15
social relationships (*wulun*), 13, 15
sovereign authority, 18, 19, 56, 80–4
storytelling, 104, 105–13, 122
supernatural, 165

television adaptations, 83
television dramas, 198
tradition of reading of, 5–6
wuxia fiction, 116
xiake, 116
See also wen
cinema and television
The Adventures of Prince Achmed (dir. Lotte Reiniger, 1926), 82
Barbie (dir. Greta Gerwig, 2024), 128–9, 146, 181
cinema adaptations, 198
Detective Dee (Chinese film series, 2015), 83
The Fellowship of the Ring (dir. Peter Jackson, 2001), 79
Harun al-Rashid (Egyptian television series, 1997), 53–4, 55–6
Harun al-Rashid (Syrian television series, 2018), 54–5
kung fu films, 116
Nirvana in Fire I (Chinese television series, 2015), 83

Nirvana in Fire II
     (Chinese television
     series, 2017), 83
Red Cliff (dir. John
     Woo, 2009), 82
Sindbad (dir. Karel
     Zeman, 1974), 126
television dramas, 12,
     83, 198
Wu Meiniang (Chinese
     television series,
     2015), 83
Wu Zetian (Chinese
     television series,
     2010–18), 83–4
'City of Brass', 166–68
Clot, André, 52
community
     alternative conceptions
          of, 99, 106
     annihilation of, 77
     belonging to, 16, 25
     break-up of, 19, 80, 99
     code of conduct, 9–10,
          12–13, 14, 25, 49,
          123
     cycle of conditions of
          good and of evil,
          176
     discourses on, 39, 46
     epic stories as to, 75
     exile from, 51
     family as, 10, 13, 16,
          18, 56–68
     future community,
          170

happiness within,
     153–65
harmony in, 9–10, 12,
     17, 18–19, 25, 45
imperfect community,
     122
incorruptible members
     of, 147
leadership of, 39–40,
     78
life within, 7, 12
love and desire within,
     17, 73, 75, 96,
     121–2, 180
loyalty within, 180
marriage and, 51
maturation into, 94
political community,
     19
preservation of, 75
redefinition of, 16, 19
reformation of, 104
restoration of harmony
     within, 27, 77,
     120–1
return to, 175
sovereign authority
     over, 14, 19, 25, 33,
     38, 46, 51, 53–4,
     80–91, 97
stories told to, 131
See also ideal
     community
comparative literature
     (Arabic/Chinese)
     adab and *wen*, 4–7

approaches to, 4
crisis in the
    humanities, 8–10
ethics of everyday
    living, and, 10–20
fiction stories, 153–4
search for paradise, 15
traditions of reading, 5
conduct
    code of conduct, 9–10,
        12–13, 14, 24, 25,
        48–51, 81, 123
    love as propriety in,
        72–5
Confucianism
    Confucian world view,
        154–5, 164, 165
    ethical ideal of
        community, 154
    ethics of living, and, 6
    human/divine
        relationship, and, 14
    individual obedience
        in all things, 154
    intelligence (*lin*), 164
    loyalty (*yi*), 164, 180
    nationalist ethos of, 165
    passion (*qing*), 164
    reason (*li*), 161
    satire of, 159, 164
    sovereign/father
        relationship, and,
        80–1
    wulun concept of
        social relationships,
        13

'Dalila al-Muhtala',
    118–19
Daoism, 155, 156, 165
daughters *See* family
desire, 44–6, 48, 72–5, 92,
    94, 95, 96, 122, 133,
    149–53, 159, 162,
    180
Detective Dee (Chinese
    film series, 2015),
    83
Di Renjie (Empress Wu's
    chancellor), 84
dystopia, 149, 153

educated men
    Confucian concept of
        conduct of, 13
    education and
        disciplining of
        desire, 149
    men uneducated in
        adab, 144
    'Muhammad the
        Foundling',
        education of, 89
    personal
        transformation
        through cultural
        education, 145–6
    See also adib; wenren
English literature, 3
epic cycles (*sira
    sha'biyya*), 5
ethics of living, 6, 7, 8,
    10–20, 16, 183

family
    absence of, 99
    alternative family, 97,
        99, 100
    break-up of, 80, 100
    brotherhood and, 100
    building of, 150
    changes to conception
        of, 104–5
    as community, 10, 13,
        16, 18, 56–68
    desire and, 17
    dysfunction within,
        99
    farewell to, 30
    harmonious family
        relations, as epitome
        of community, 18
    Harun al-Rashid
        stories, and, 18
    inclusion within, 160
    jealousy and, 31
    kingly family, 77
    loyalty within, 68–72
    marriage and, 51, 97,
        101
    merger with polity and
        with society, 56
    modern idea of
        'nuclear' family,
        104
    motherhood and, 81
    murder of family
        members, 110
    parental duty of care as
        to, 84, 97
    paternal authority as
        foundation of
        political authority,
        105, 108
    paternal political
        authority within, 107
    plotting against, 117
    proper conduct as
        foundation for
        parental authority,
        81–2
    redefinition of, 16, 19
    reinforcement of
        relations in, 101
    restoration of harmony
        within, 27
    reunification of, 76,
        102, 141, 143
    society and, 105
    sovereign authority
        over, 53, 105
    time for, 14
    as wealth, 16
    See also marriage
al-Farabi, 40–1, 43, 44, 94,
    103, 123, 153
fathers See family
Fellowship of the Ring,
    79
film See cinema and
    television
'The Fisherman and the
    Demon', 24, 25,
    30–4, 41, 43, 44,
    45–6, 48, 61, 63, 66,
    67, 68, 151

fitna, 50, 130, 138, 139,
        143
food, 128, 141, 144–5
freedom
    Confucianist/Daoist
        concept of, 148, 155
    of expression, 182
    friendship and, 105
    happiness and, 164
    paradise and, 148–9
    search for, 15
friendship
    adab and, 103
    Confucianist concept
        of, 105
    family and, 104–7, 109,
        110, 118, 121

good life *See joie de vivre*
Guan Yu, 109

Hadith, *adab* and, 6
Han Fei, 105
Haohan, 110–11, 113,
        116, 117–18, 120,
        121
happiness
    within community,
        153–65
    freedom and, 164
    meaning and, 17, 20
harmony 18, 27
Harry Potter (Rowling),
        80, 94–5, 97–8,
        99–100, 119–20,
        125, 178–80

Harun al-Rashid
    'Aladdin with Moles
        on His Cheeks', and,
        115–16, 120
    'Ali b. Bakkar and
        Shams al-Nahar',
        and, 64–5
    'Anis al-Jalis and Nur
        al-Din b. Khaqan',
        and, 65–8
    cultural influence and
        legacy of, 53
    Dalila al-Muhtala, and,
        119
    Emperor Taizong, and,
        3
    family in community,
        theme of, 68–72
    Harry Potter and,
        119
    'The Hunchback', and,
        145
    ideal community, and,
        150
    joie de vivre, and, 130
    justice and injustice,
        and, 120
    King Solomon, and,
        10–20, 52, 60, 64,
        68, 123, 145, 182
    Kitab al-aghani, and,
        56–9
    The Lord of the Rings
        and, 119
    love and passion in
        just rule, 123

love as kingly
    genealogy, 75–7
love as propriety in
    conduct, 72–5
loyalty in love, 68–72
modern tyrants, 119
'Muhammad the
    Foundling and
    Harun al-Rashid',
    84–9
popular epic stories,
    in, 114
'The Porter and the
    Three Ladies of
    Baghdad', 62–4
scholarly rehabilitation
    of, 52–3
shuttar and, 120
stories of, 52
'The Story of Ashraf
    and Anjab', and,
    89–91
'The Story of Jullanar',
    97
television productions
    as to, 53–6
Thousand and One
    Nights, and, 53,
    56–60, 114, 148
'The Three Apples',
    and, 60–1
'The Two Viziers', and,
    144, 145
tyranny of, 52
Hasan Shuman, 113, 114,
    118

'Hasib Karim al-Din', 80,
    91, 125–6, 151, 166,
    168–70, 173–4, 175,
    176
heroes
    Arabic literature, 80
    Haohan, 110–11, 113,
        116, 117–18, 120,
        121
'The Hunchback', 145

Ibn al-Jawzi, 38, 39, 41,
    42, 159
Ibn Khaldun, 6
iconization of rulers, 81,
    83, 84, 150
ideal community
    alternative conceptions
        of, 19, 98
    building of, 17, 57, 79,
        148, 150
    code of conduct, 18,
        24–34, 48, 81
    disillusion with, 153
    dreams of, 12
    form of, 154
    imaginings of, 15, 16,
        104, 106, 149
    limits of, 151
    love and desire within,
        46
    moral beauty, and, 129,
        150
    politics of, 175
    power, justice, and
        reason within, 48

proper love within, 46
real world, in, 145,
    181–2
reason (*'aql*) and, 41,
    94, 122
resemblance to, 159
sovereign's conduct as
    to, 14
transformation into,
    147
yearning for, 20, 152
Ihsan 'Abd al-Quddus, 3
immortality, 16, 161, 172
Islam, 3, 12, 38, 53, 72,
    73, 78, 102, 112,
    152–3, 167, 170
Israel-Palestine conflict, 9

joie de vivre (good life)
    adab and, 183
    ethical life, 16
    life as a banquet, 20
    material and literary
        forms of, 128–30
    propriety and, 10, 125
Journey to the West, 158
'Jullanar', 91–8, 151,
    156–9, 161, 162

Khalid b al-Walid, 3
king *See* sovereign
'King Yunan and Sage
    Duban', 31
'The King's Son and the
    She-Ghoul', 31
Klonsky, Milton, 52

leadership of community,
    39–40, 78
Li Bai, 124
Li Chaowei, 160
life
    meaning of, 20, 126,
        148, 175
    See also community;
        ideal community;
        joie de vivre
Liu Bei, 108
Liu Yi, 159– 65
The Lord of the Rings
    (Tolkien), 21–4,
    48–9, 79–80, 94–5,
    97–8, 99–100,
    119–20, 125, 149
love
    within community (*see*
        community; ideal
        community)
    justice and, 123
    as kingly genealogy,
        75–7
    loyalty and, 24, 68–72
    meaning of, 67, 72,
        77
    passion and, 123
    as propriety in
        conduct, 72–5

magic, 21, 23, 28, 29, 45,
    80, 147, 158, 168,
    172, 173, 177
Mahfouz, Naguib, 147,
    150, 176

marriage
    into family, 97, 101
    in relation to
        community and to
        family, 51
    See also family
meaning
    generating of, 135
    happiness and, 17, 20
    of life, 20, 126, 148, 175
    of love, 67, 72, 77
    paradoxical, 149–53
    purpose and, 9–10, 15
    simultaneous presence
        of opposite
        meaning, 143
men *See* family; *shuttar*
Mencius, 105
'The Merchant and the
    Genie', 24, 25–30,
    151
Middle Kingdom (China),
    156
mothers *See* family
Muhammad ʿAbd
    al-Rahman Yunus,
    52
'Muhammad the
    Foundling and
    Harun al-Rashid'
    84–9
Muqaddima (Ibn
    Khaldun), 6
al-Muʿtasim, 86
myths
    Chinese literature, 155

    purpose of, 12
    reinterpretations of, 15
    transformation into, 12

Nights See Thousand and
    One Nights
Nirvana in Fire I (Chinese
    television series,
    2015), 83
Nirvana in Fire II
    (Chinese television
    series, 2017), 83
novels and stories,
    distinction between,
    10–20
'Nur al-Din al-Misri and
    Badr al-Din al-Basri'
    See 'The Two Viziers'

obedience, 34, 44, 105, 113
oppression, 36, 40,
othering, 9, 182
Outlaws of the Marsh See
    Water Margin

paradise
    children of, 136
    freedom and, 148–9
    reward of, 85
    search for, 15
parents *See* family
politics
    community, 19, 175
    merger of political and
        social realms, 13
    paternal, 105, 107, 108

'The Porter and the Three
    Ladies of Baghdad'
    62–4

Qisas al-anbiya', 49,
    150–1, 166
qualities, 34–48, 112–3, 117
Qur'an, 14, 49, 78, 86, 166

reading, traditions of, 5–6
Red Cliff (dir. John Woo,
    2009), 82
relationships *See* social
    relationships
religions, 7, 12, 14, 15, 16;
    See also Buddhism;
    Confucianism;
    Daoism; Islam
Robin Hood, 111
Rowling, J. K., 178–80

satire
    adab, 134–8
    Confucianism, 159, 164
    storytelling, 130, 134, 143
service, 13, 105, 117, 154
'The Seven Voyages of
    Sindbad the Sailor',
    2, 125–8, 147,
    149–50, 151, 177
Shi Gongan (novel), 1, 2
shuttar, 112, 114, 115,
    118, 120, 121
sira sha'biyya (epic
    cycles), 5
Sirat 'Antara, 80

*Sirat al-Amira Dhat
    al-Himma*, 80
social relationships
    absence of harmony
        within, 121
    breaking down of,
        marital infidelity as
        cause of, 27
    Confucian concept of
        wulun, 13
    friendship as
        framework for
        sovereign/subject
        relationship, 105
    harmony and, 121
    love and loyalty as
        cornerstones of, 24
    meaning and, 71
society *See* community
Solomon, King
    'The City of Brass',
        and, 166–72
    conflict between
        passion and reason,
        180–1
    conflict between love
        and desire, 9
    death of, 25, 49, 169,
        172, 173, 174
    desire for women, 50–1
    ethics of living, and,
        10–20, 180
    Harun al-Rashid
        stories, and, 10–20,
        52, 60, 64, 68, 123,
        145, 182

King David's
    judgement as to
    field, 78
The Lord of the Rings,
    and, 21–4, 48–9
power of, 21, 175
Qur'an and, 78
Solomon's ring, 48–50
Song Jiang, 121
source of his power, 21
'The story of Hasib
    Karim al-Din', and,
    173–7
*Thousand and One
    Nights*, and, 24–5,
    30–1, 34–5, 45, 68,
    77, 130, 147, 150–1
wisdom of Solomon,
    174–5
Song Huizong, Emperor,
    106–10
sons *See* family
sovereign authority, 14,
    19, 25, 33, 38, 46,
    51, 53–4, 80–91, 97
Sperl, Stefan, 6
'The Story of Ashraf and
    Anjab' 89–91
storytelling
    Arabic literature, 100,
        122, 125, 128, 151,
        180–1
    Chinese literature, 104,
        105–13, 122
    efficacy of, 130, 143
    friendship in, 104, 122

and *joie de vivre*, 128
listening and, 126
modern, 128
morality and, 145
occasions (assemblies),
    125, 130
satire of, 130, 134, 143
and self-discovery, 125
silence and, 143
tension between ideal
    and real, 128
strong men *See shuttar*
Sun Quan, 108

Taizong, Emperor, 3
'Taj al-Muluk and Dunya',
    71–5, 76
*Tales of the Marvellous
    and News of the
    Strange*, 84, 91
al-Tawhidi, Abu Hayyan,
    103, 104, 109, 117,
    121, 122
television *See* cinema and
    television
*Thousand and One
    Nights*
    and Arabic epics,
        113–16
    beauty within, 129
    as literature or as folk
        tales, 5
    code of conduct, 24
    equivalent Chinese
        characters, 3–4
    and ethics of living, 10

love and desire within, 24
meaning of life, 148
morality and, 145
rewriting of, 147
stories within, 27
television adaptation, 55
tragedy within, 30
'The Three Apples', 60–1
'The Two Viziers', 144
Three Kingdoms (Luo Guanzhong), 82, 106–10, 117
Tolkien, J.R.R., 21, 48

'Umar b. al-Khattab, the second of the Guided Caliphs, 59
''Umar al-Nu'man and His Two Sons', 69–77, 79, 80
utopia, 18, 149, 152, 153

vices and virtues, 38

Water Margin, 110–13, 117–18, 120, 121, 122
wen
    adab and, 4–7
    Confucianist ethics of living, and, 6

definition of, 6–7
relevance to modern world, 7
Wu Meiniang (Chinese television series, 2015), 83
Wu Song, 117
Wu Zetian (Chinese television series, 2010–18), 83–4
Wu Zetian, Empress, 83
wulun
    as central theme in this book, 17
    Confucian concept of, 13
    ethics of living, and, 15
    modern redefinition of family, and, 104
    network of social relationships, 13, 80–1

Xue, General, 3
Xue family, 1–2

Yusuf al-Siba'i, 3

Zaydan, Jurji, 3
Zhang Fei, 109
Zoroastrians, 32
Zubayda, 55, 81, 84, 85, 86, 88, 89, 97

World of Islam

The World of Islam series aims to provide non-specialist readers with a reliable and balanced overview of the diverse manifestations of Islam. It seeks to redress misperceptions by offering a nuanced survey of the plurality of interpretations amongst Muslims around the world and through-out history, who express their faith and values through varied cultural, social, intellectual and religious means. Covering themes pertinent to Muslims and non-Muslims alike, the civiliza-tional series approach encourages readers to delve into the commonalities as well as the distinctions that define different Muslim traditions. In access-ible language and concise format, these books deliver well-researched yet easy-to-follow intro-ductions that will stimulate readers to think differently about Islam.

Be inspired by the World of Islam.

The Institute of Ismaili Studies

The Institute of Ismaili Studies, established in 1977, has an extensive programme of multilingual and interdisciplinary research and publications. Informed by rigorous scholarly research, we endeavour to make available texts relating to Islam and Muslim communities in their historical and contemporary contexts. Our focus is on Ismaili and related Shi'i studies, Qur'anic studies, and also Islam's diverse devotional, literary, intellectual, artistic, and esoteric traditions. Many of these publications highlight the relationship of faith and practice to broader dimensions of society, culture, and modern life.

IIS publications take the form of monographs; critical editions and translations of significant primary or secondary texts; edited volumes and conference proceedings; reference works such as bibliographies, manuscript catalogues, and encyclopaedias; occasional papers and essays; and trade non-fiction works aimed at lay audiences.

Authors of the Institute's publications hail from various parts of the world and express a range of views and ideas, which are not necessarily those of the Institute itself.

A full list of the publications of the Institute of Ismaili Studies can be found on our website at www.iis.ac.uk.